BULLYING
IN PLAIN
SIGHT

BULLYING
IN PLAIN
SIGHT

*How Inattentive Adults Encourage
the School Bullies*

Dr. Dan Chandler

TATE PUBLISHING
AND **ENTERPRISES**, LLC

Published by Tate Publishing & Enterprises, LLC
127 E. Trade Center Terrace | Mustang, Oklahoma 73064 USA
1.888.361.9473 | www.tatepublishing.com

Tate Publishing is committed to excellence in the publishing industry. The company reflects the philosophy established by the founders, based on Psalm 68:11,
"The Lord gave the word and great was the company of those who published it."

Published in the United States of America

ISBN: 978-1-68207-092-5
1. Education / Administration / General
2. Education / Decision-Making & Problem Solving
15.10.16

Acknowledgments

The author would like to acknowledge the scholarly efforts of his three dedicated student researchers at The College of New Jersey: Alyssa Laird, Belicia Perry-Green, and Taylor Prall.

These three ladies will be excellent teachers because of their humanistic qualities. They helped greatly to understand girl vs. girl bullying as well.

Contents

Preface

We did not write this book for a scientific journal, so we did not feel compelled to have all the appropriate footnotes and bibliography. It sounds cynical, but many people in universities as well as experts on TV who speak and write about education spent a very short time actually in the classrooms, hallways, cafeterias, and gyms. They took one look and said, "Get me out of here. I'm going to a university and write for journals and tell parents and schools how they should be dealing with bullying." We were actually there for many years talking to kids and helping victims and bullies alike. Our opinion is that there is no publication out there that approaches bullying from the standpoint that this book does. Everyone feels that ample supervision is effective supervision. We will show in this book that such a notion may be farther from the truth than you might realize.

So if you are looking for annotated bibliographies and copious footnotes, you won't find them in this book. We have given credit where it's due, but the revelations in this book are principally derived from careful observation and talking to students face-to-face. Some of the ways that bullying can occur and how it occurs with supervision close by may amaze you; but it is all true. This message needed to get out, not sent to a scientific journal review panel who returns it six times for revisions. We did not write it to impress the people in the ivory tower—they usually don't go near an actual school anyway, because it's easier to write about it from a safe distance. We wrote this book for administrators, school board members, and teachers who are practitioners and have only a few minutes each day to actually read something before rushing off to other responsibilities. In this book, we make suggestions for improvement that can be implemented tomorrow, and we have done so by first pointing out what the average person simply does not see. Deal with it. It could be your child who is the target of a bully today.

Introduction

This work is for parents, scholars, administrators, school board members, lawyers, politicians, media personalities, the police, and mental health professionals, all of whom think they really know what is going on in the school building on any given day. Unfortunately, not all of them do. You heard me correctly. The politicians who think anyone can teach or administrate without specific school training but with an advanced degree are alarmingly clueless, and it is the physical and emotional health of both the children and adults that is at stake. Some, on the lunatic fringe, think teachers and administrators should be carrying firearms in the school—forget the protocols that a trained law officer must follow before he pulls his trigger, or the explanations needed if a single military bullet is expended. These people who also want a child found with a nail file expelled from school permanently are also operating sans clue. But I digress.

The unhappy truth is that the average adult, even those who work closely with young people in the schools, cannot grasp the amount of random and nonrandom bullying that occurs daily—often as if on schedule and at a degree to which a bullied child's life during a school day is turned into a living hell, sometimes culminating in suicide. A lot of important people nationally and locally have weighed in on the subject, including the President and the First Lady, legislators, entertainers like Lady Gaga, mental health professionals, religious leaders, law enforcement experts, mental health professionals, guidance counselors, parents, and children, although sadly, input from the children often comes too late because they are too afraid to say anything, lest they get victimized yet again by the bullies. Despite the media's fascination with electronic forms of bullying, having to just get to school, navigate the hallways, dress in the locker room, eat in the cafeteria, sit (yes, just plain *sit*!) in the classroom, and get home safely and incident-free each day is frightening for many children; and most suffer in silence because they think they will be even more at risk from the angry bully if they report the matter to a responsible adult. And they know that a solution like, "Let's all sit down and talk this matter out" is inherently unfair to the victim.

You might be asking the question, How can this be happening if my child goes to a "good" school in a "good" school district where there is, for example, "good" and ample supervision designed to prevent such things from happening? Where are these "bad guys?" Are they sneaking around and hiding in clever places where the highly skilled supervisors can't find them? Our assertion in this book—and we provide many real-life examples that, in a moment of honesty, your child might agree with—is that while some of the bullying may be surreptitious, most of it occurs in plain sight of the supervisors, sometimes a mere few feet from where they are standing. Impossible, you say? How can a diligent adult supervising the playground, the cafeteria, the auditorium, the playing field/gym/locker room, or their own teaching space let bullying occur right under their proverbial noses and not see it? Easy. Get your notebook out—this will be a bumpy ride.

That is the purpose of this book. Here we have taken every place children can go during the school day, from the time they leave the house till they return, and we give many examples of scenarios of how the bullying occurs, and assert why we think it can happen—often even more effectively—when there are adult supervisors around.

The media gets goose bumps about cyber bullying because it has more intrigue to it. But in the school zeitgeist, insults of a racial, ethnic, sexual, and disability nature are passed back and forth all day long at close range, and go unheard of by the supervisor and unreported by the victim. Things are being whispered in your child's ear or stated openly right in the middle of the hallway every class change, causing children great stress and dread, and making them, for example, always late to class as the child takes the "long way" to class to avoid the bully, or group of bullies, or strangely misses the bus in the morning a lot because he or she goes the "long way," if at all, to the stop. Merely going to school at all quickly loses its appeal, especially when a child "looks different" in some way— whether because of physical size and shape (e.g., too thin, too well developed or underdeveloped as a female, disabled, overweight), clothing, skin color, ethnicity, socioeconomic background, sexual preference, religion, and so on AD infinitum. Girls get propositioned and harassed sexually to the point that someone would be sued in a workplace for the same behavior. Children who are overweight are verbally and physically abused every day; someone of color or ethnicity will hear constant derogatory comments. The adults standing nearby will not hear them.

After thirty-plus years in schools and having a relationship with students in such a way that they would actually tell me as the adult what is *really* happening, combined with stories shared by my college students, you can read of these tragic incidents, virtually all of which occur in plain sight. Later, some thoughts about prevention strategies will be discussed and how, sadly, many of them are simply window dressing, and therefore completely ineffectual.

1

Toward a Definition of Bullying

The government has a website named stopbullying.gov. Here is the definition they provide for *bullying*:

> Bullying is unwanted, aggressive behavior among school aged children that involves a real or perceived power imbalance. The behavior is repeated, or has the potential to be repeated, over time. Both kids who are bullied and who bully others may have serious, lasting problems...

The definition continues:

> In order to be considered bullying, the behavior must be aggressive and include:
>
> An Imbalance of Power – Kids who bully use their power—such as physical strength, access to embarrassing information, or popularity—to control or harm others. Power imbalances can change over time and in different situations, even if they involve the same people.

> Repetition – Bullying behaviors happen more than once or have the potential to happen more than once.

Then the definition ends this way: "Bullying includes actions such as making threats, spreading rumors, attacking someone physically or verbally, and excluding someone from a group on purpose."

....

For any educational organization, definitions can be cumbersome and tricky things, often filled with inconvenient truths and budgetary implications. Let's begin with a definition of bullying that makes a logical *a priori* claim—that *bullying is VIOLENCE*—and not, for example, kids being kids, or, if you will, a rite of passage, or a practical joke. This definition is a definition of *violence*, and it is an expansive one; and as we have recently seen in the news with definitions of children with autism spectrum disorder, for example, a simple change of a cumbersome definition can instantly lower costs, lighten a school's responsibility and liability, require less staff, turn negative statistics into promising ones, and, as in the case of incidents of bullying, make a school a much safer place overnight—on paper at least!

Here is a definition of *violence* offered by Dr. Mona Moore from the Anti-Bullying Centre of the Education Department of Trinity College, Dublin, Ireland.

Violence is aggressive behavior, that may be physically, sexually, or emotionally abusive. The aggressive behavior is conducted by an individual or group against another, or others. Physically abusive behavior is where a child, adolescent, or group directly or indirectly ill-treats, injures, or kills another or others—or we would add, causes the person to take their own life. The aggressive behavior can involve pushing, shoving, shaking, punching, kicking, squeezing, burning, or any other form of physical assault on a person(s) or on property. Emotionally abusive behavior is where there are verbal attacks, threats, taunts, slagging, mocking, yelling, exclusion, and malicious rumors. Sexually abusive behavior is where there is sexual assault or rape.

We also would add, and offer as the principal thrust of this book, that it need not be repeated before the definition kicks in, so to speak, and it is aided and abetted by well-meaning or intellectually and/or emotionally lazy adults who lack discernment, which makes any efforts at proactiveness largely ineffectual.

At this point, we insert some illustrations that will begin to paint the picture as to why, in most schools, bullying occurs under the radar, yet in plain sight, and how this bullying is aided and abetted by the actions, ignorance, or the lack of action on the part of adults.

Sometime in your life you watched—perhaps as a child, or with your children—a Charlie Brown (*Peanuts*) one-hour special on TV. They were always superbly done, and often included subtle humor that adults could appreciate with easy listening jazz piano playing in the background. However, do you remember how adults—or more precisely, the voices of invisible adults were depicted? The sound was that of a muted trumpet going *Wanh-wanh- wanh-wa-wa-wanh-wa-wanh*, to which Peppermint Patty or another child would answer, "Yes, ma'am!" The adults were always invisible, and they spoke an entirely different language. The children were in their own world. As were the adults.

On other occasions, you may have read the comic strip *Calvin and Hobbes*, where Hobbes, a mere, small stuffed tiger when in the presence of adults became to young Calvin a life-sized tiger standing on hind legs and communicating as a close confidant with the boy when the grown-ups were not around.

Finally, you may remember the old Star Trek series where the Captain, the Doctor, and, of course, Spock, were always beaming down to a strange planet's surface with several gratuitous crew members who you knew would be expendable before the show was over. In one of the episodes, the group beams down, and their scanners show that there is a life-form present, but it is apparently invisible. The intelligent life-form turns out to be the rocks that were moving so slow that the humans could not perceive the movement, and the humans were imperceptible to the rocks because they, the humans, were moving too fast.

Okay, enough picture painting. Let's see if an actual point can be made here. When we speak of bullying occurring under the radar, one type of bullying in this category would be cyberbullying, a favorite of the media but for the most part clearly out of the control of school officials even though, since someone must be blamed, the school becomes the sacrificial lamb in this instance.

We are not talking about cyberbullying in this book. The bullying of which we speak is the kind that occurs virtually right in front of adults inside the school, and because the life-forms around those adults are different and speak a different language, the adults are completely unable to perceive the bullying that is happening due to indifference, low emotional intelligence, a lack of simple empathy, or decontextualized supervisory skills, or perhaps they are not willing to acknowledge that bullying is occurring because of a narrow definition they subscribe to, such as that, "it is not bullying if someone is not physically assaulting another person in plain sight." Or a more popular twist: "It's not bullying if there is no established pattern of bullying (!)." Or finally: "*Our* Kids don't behave like that…what do you think our community is, the Inner City?"

Imagine that reasoning being applied to rape or child molestation, for example. *Decontextualized* in this sense could mean an able-bodied teacher or hallway monitor—perhaps one that is large and in charge with a booming voice, like the football coach, or one whose mere presence can strike fear in the hearts of students and would-be bullies, yet one who cannot or will not perceive or anticipate trouble spots or problems before they happen—a significant problem that we will speak to in this book. Here are some facts about bullying that may surprise you. This list was compiled by the Four H Clubs of Kentucky:

An estimated 160,000 students miss school every day due to a fear of bullying or harassment.

Bullying causes fear and creates a climate of disrespect in schools. It has a negative impact on student learning.

There appears to be a strong relationship between bullying as a youth and experiencing legal and criminal issues as an adult. One study showed 60% of those characterized as a bully in grades 6–9 had one or more criminal convictions by age 24.

The National Threat Assessment Center found that the attackers in more than 2/3 of 37 mass school shootings felt "persecuted, bullied threatened, attacked, or injured by others" and used this as their motivation for seeking revenge.

Recent surveys show that American Children 8–15 years of age rate bullying as a greater problem than racism, sexual pressure, or the use of drugs and alcohol.

Bullying peaks in middle school and starts to decline in high school. However, it never completely disappears.

Boys tend to bully boys and girls, while girls tend to bully other girls.

In middle school, boys who are more passive or less physically mature than their peers are often the target of bullies. Girls who are physically mature early are most often the target of bullies.

In the Maine Project against Bullying, 80% of adolescents and 90% of students from the fourth to eighth grade reported being bullied at school. In the same study, 71% of the students asserted that the teachers or other adults in the building or classroom ignored the bullying incidents. Willingly ignoring the incident is not what the responders meant—that would be unconscionable behavior and criminal on the part of people who work in the school. *Ignoring* in this instance refers to a complete lack of awareness or anticipatory awareness—stated simply, a complete lack of discernment that the bulling was even going on.

Another group of adults and students that has been identified in the literature are the *bystanders*. Suzanne SooHoo (3) refers to the praxis of these individuals as bystanderism. *Bystanderism*, as defined by SooHoo, is the response of people who observe something that demands intervention on their part but they choose not to get involved. Out on the street, there is no law requiring anyone to do anything to help their fellowman. Law school questions always have an Olympic swimmer looking out at the ocean to a child that is drowning and ask what the swimmer can be charged with for ignoring the drowning child. The answer: nothing. It's purely a matter of conscience as to whether one chooses to help his or her fellowman. You can't be blamed for not helping a person. How often have we seen someone in New York City, for example, being beaten by thugs while average people on the street calmly keep on walking? Bystanders are involved in the newest strategies to end bullying. Up to now, since the law requires nothing of a bystander, the bystander has gotten a free pass, so to speak.

Often, these folks will get involved, but often selectively, and without any context, as when they might yell "Keep it down, you people!" when things get too loud. Or, "If I hear a peep out of any of you, you are all going to the office!" Thus, whether it is an involved traffic cop in the hallway or the selectively involved bystander, their efforts appear effective to the detached observer, but they amount to decontextualized generalizations that impose no punishment on the bully or give to the victim. More will be said about the emerging role of the bystander in the daily drama that is bullying.

Did you know that in many places in the world—England, for example—bullying in the workplace is against the law? However, in America, the leader who, like John Wayne in battle, "kicks butt and calls names" is the one who is revered by the media. Is it any wonder that you still hear people complain that being too picky about all of this bullying stuff in schools is turning us all into a nation of Prius-driving wimps? That is a common theme from "conservative" radio entertainers and Tea Party aficionados. They still reason that it is all a rite of passage that all children must go through, and that they will be stronger for the experience.

2

What Is Decontextualized
Supervision?

Let's give you an example of decontextualized supervision from your childhood, assuming you had brothers or sisters. Do you remember a scenario resembling this one? You are twelve years old, and you are in your bedroom working on your important sixth-grade geography project, where you are gluing figures and trees and other scenery on, say, a shadow box. Alternatively, let's say you are working diligently on your stamp collection, with neat little piles spaced across your desk. Your little brother or sister (this might have been *you* doing it to your brother or sister!) sneaks up behind you and makes a fake sneeze, blowing air across your work; or he or she bumps your arm, causing your work to go flying all over the place.

You turn around and punch your brother and yell at him to "get out of here, you brat!" And he runs out of your room screaming even bloodier murder than usual to your parents who are downstairs relaxing and getting a few precious moments away from all of you crazy young people after a particularly trying day. Your mother or your father screams up at you to "get down here, young man/lady!" And they ask you this question: "What have I told you about hitting your little brother?" (He, of course, is standing there taking loud heaving breaths and looking especially pathetic.) You know the rest. You say, "He messed up my project!" Which is followed by the mandatory bunch of "Did toos" and "Did-nots," "It was an accident," "You did it on purpose," etc.

Your father/mother, unable to perceive the truth-teller, ends this "discussion" with the warning that he or she better not hear a "peep" out of either of you the rest of the night, or you will both be grounded for a week. And then you are told to go clean up your project and not to ever hit your brother again, and how you should know better because you are older, blah blah blah—all of which goes in one ear and out the other because it is adultspeak and it's another language being spoken and it sounds to you like *Wanh-wanh-wanh* from the Charlie Brown special anyway. You know, where the words of the adults are always the sound of an unintelligible muted trumpet. As you walk away, your brother is grinning at you, and you shake a fist at him. The end result—peace and quiet in the house, as Bill Cosby states in his video on parenthood. Parents don't want justice; they want quiet! In the example, no actual justice was meted out, and you as the aggrieved person start asking yourself, as many victims do, *What's the use of reporting this since I have a bigger burden placed upon me by doing so?*

It is *decontextualized supervision* that may keep people from serious bodily injury and perhaps keep you safe in the event of a fire or some other emergency, but because it ends in the well-known detached or lazy man's pretend-to-be-a-tough-guy tactic known as *false equivalency* (4), where both the perpetrator and the victim are treated as equal warring factions, your problem goes unresolved, as your boss ends his discussion with the two of you by saying, "Now I want the two of you to behave like gentlemen and fix this problem, or else…Now get out of here!"

Perhaps you have seen this in the workplace if you have an unaware, lazy, or particularly cowardly boss who, in true Machiavellian style, always considers the political weight of the people involved in the problem before deciding how to act or whom to proact upon. So you, the new person on the block, who may be completely correct in your complaint to the boss about the other person's bullying behavior, will be treated as though the whole problem was an even fight between two angry people because the other person—the actual bully—has some political clout in the organization or the town. This is how bullies live to bully another day, and how most bullying may never go away, no matter how much your "good" school district brags about the special steps they have taken to prevent bullying, often after the fact or being mandated by the state legislature.

Excursus: The Nizkor Project's Logic Fallacies

When you have a moment, look up "the Nizkor Project" on your computer and read from their list of logic fallacies that people in all walks of life use every day.

Here is an example: the "post hoc ergo propter hoc" logic fallacy. This is where a solution to a problem is tried and it appears to have amazing results. The solution receives rave reviews for its seeming effectiveness. Case closed. So after the advent of the bicycle helmet laws in every state, the percentage of head injuries in children riding bicycles has been reduced almost 80%! Who can argue with such a great statistic? However, ask yourself this question: How many children do you actually see out there riding bikes in your neighborhood anymore? Either because of the over-organization of kids' play with organized leagues down to five years of age, or the overcautious approach to child care, where parents these days never let the child out of their sight and arrange play dates like visits to the dentist, or children in afterschool programs with no access to a bike because their parents must work and the child will not be home till six from the after-school care program. Whatever the reason, there are over 80% less kids actually riding a bike on your tree-lined street than there were thirty years ago. Do you still think helmets should get all the credit for less head injuries?

Okay, that is one example of a logic fallacy. Here is the one that we speak of numerous times in this book: the false equivalence logic fallacy. Often, it is used by the media in this way to stir the pot and create viewer interest. A respected scientist provides the result of his work on, say, global warming, to Wolf Blitzer on CNN one night. Mr. Blitzer then switches this point-counterpoint pseudo discussion to, for example, Ann Coulter, who proceeds to laugh at the scientist and call him names. What's the fallacy? The scientist who has spent years developing this theory and Ann Coulter are treated as though both have the same scholarly and academic standing to be offering opinions about the topic of global warming. The average viewer looks at this as a fair fight, entered into by two equal warring factions, and that both have intelligent information to dispense to the listening audience on the topic. What you believe about global warming is beside the point. The fallacy comes from trying to have an intelligent discussion without two equally intelligent individuals opining on the topic. This is a favorite among the media when it comes to point-counterpoint discussions.

Here are two quick examples of how the false equivalence logic fallacy plays out in school:

Your child gets pushed in the hallway, and his books go flying. He yells at the assailant to "cut it out, you dork!" A teacher comes upon the scene and screams, "Knock it off, you two, before I send both of your sorry butts to the office.

Now get out of here before I drag you down to the office!" Thus your child and the bully are treated like two equal warring factions who both need to be yelled at for acting inappropriately in the hallway.

Here is a far worse (or better) example: Following an incidence of bullying where your child has been getting unmercifully picked on for some time, he or she fights back, and both children are sent to the guidance counselor, who talks to the children about their aggressive and hostile interactions and makes them apologize to one another and shake hands and "calmly talk things out." Thus the counselor has treated both individuals the same, with no effort made to find out who actually started all this trouble in the first place. False equivalence logic fallacy strikes again! Your boss will do this to you when the day comes that you finally give an annoying veteran coworker who plays golf with the boss a piece of your mind. You will remember this page as he tells the both of you that he expects both of you to act more professionally or heads will roll. "Now get back to work, you two clowns!"

....

Now back to our story...

Another example of decontextualized supervision or selective supervision occurs with specific groups of students, like students of color, or girls as opposed to boys. Recently, Chinese students were the targets of severe bullying in a predominantly black high school in Philadelphia. The superintendent, a black woman, began by saying in a somewhat agitated and slightly frantic way to the press, "We do not have a racial problem in this school!" The efforts at evenhandedness that school officials and elected officials use to be politically correct, though well intentioned, provide, as in the Bill Cosby example, no actual justice for the victims. That can be seen in the stopbullying. gov definition, which never specifically mentions how girls and boys bully differently, the parents' responsibility, or the inadequate supervision by even the best-intentioned school employees.

Even the trained guidance counselors are slower to lay blame and report the misdeed to the office, choosing instead, as pointed out above, to have the "warring factions" sit down and talk things out—another example of false equivalence. The targeted students have no interest—nor should they have any interest in sitting down around a table and talking out their "differences" with someone who had as their intention to give this poor victim a pounding in the first place. The guidance counselor typically does not want to be seen as one who turns people into the office, as it is considered to be un-counselorlike behavior, and a guarantee that no student will share any further secrets with him or her because the grapevine will see to it that no one comes to the counselor who is a snitch.

Adults in the schools tend to be—dare we say it—clueless when it comes to anticipating bullying behavior. Police are trained to spot problem situations prior to their occurrence. The experience of teachers is that their involvement often comes after the event, and the actions they take are often too generalized. This is why any talk of arming teachers in schools with guns is a horrible idea. Who will they shoot if two parents are going after one another physically or with weapons? How will they know how and when to do it? Their scores at the firing range are irrelevant! Where's Charlton Heston now?

Schools are that way also; they react to a serious problem with programs and speakers and assemblies that are wonderful for publicity to let the world know that the district means business, but as is usually the case, individual victims are denied justice. The "experts" always work outside of education. No college course prepares aspiring teachers with the skills needed to be proactive in dealing with bullying, let alone carrying a firearm. Often, the school district brings in mental health professionals who are wise in their disciplines but have no concept of how a school actually functions and the human interactions that occur each day. When the world looks at schools and their problems, they are always quick to pick someone *not* from the schools or with a small amount of experience in schools to be the "fixer," whether this is the new secretary of education who was a lawyer or CEO, or sometimes the superintendent who was an ex-general, so "he'll be sure to shape this place up, by God!"

Every year we see some new hot name in education, who never spent a day actually teaching in a school, saying bold things. Michelle Rhee, one of the latest hot names in education, for example, taught for three years. Arne Duncan, President Obama's secretary of education, never taught; he's an "expert," though. Fascinating stuff, but let's stay on task…

Here's an example of how the expert from someplace else does not understand the human dynamics of a high school. Do you know why many students stay after school every day and look busy as they flutter around the hallways, often till 5:00 p.m. and beyond? Hang on, you aren't expecting what comes next: Young people fall in love. You already knew that, of course; but sometimes they fall in love with someone whom Mom or Dad would not approve of because of a variety of things, not the least of which could be things related to race, religion, age, or gender, for example—as in a consenting homosexual relationship or the romantic interactions of transgender students. Some people know that even showing up in the neighborhood with someone "different" might be a big problem, so the school provides a convenient place—with all of its nooks, crannies, stairwells, and open doors for all kinds of things being tacitly permitted to occur. The mental health professionals from the county do not know this, I assure you. Maybe you don't either. Time to become more aware of what is really going on, folks! Still thinking that all you need to be able to teach kids is high grades in your disciplines and advanced degrees? Read on, all of you "experts."

Another "expert" is the architect who invariably designs a school with banks of, say, three hundred lockers at the corners of corridors because it makes for a very aesthetically pleasing appearance with no lockers in a large part of the hallways. Before the improvement, one monitor at the end of a hallway could tell, while classes are going on and the halls are mostly clear, whether someone was in the hallway, looking several hundred feet in two directions at a right angle. Now the trouble is happening in the small locker alcoves and cannot be seen at a distance, only up close, requiring more adult supervision that the school district is not thrilled about having to pay for. Faced with having to add more hall supervisors, brilliant school board members will sometimes agree to add a half-time supervisor so they do not have to pay the person benefits. Let's see you try to cover the hallways for the *entire* day with a half-time person! I tried it…even with mirrors, it doesn't work! Many school boards are perfectly content to have their highest paid-employee in the building—the principal—doing regular hall duty because the board does not want to pay $12 an hour to a hall monitor.

A big part of any teacher's day is the time spent out of their teaching area; the cafeteria and the hallways are examples of places where a lot of trouble is brewing, and many don't see it, or they choose not to acknowledge it. Some even take the long way around to avoid the problem area.

Perhaps this course might serve as Awareness 101 for readers as we talk about the places in the building where bullying occurs and some of the acts of bullying that are happening every day—below the radar of the adults who are supposed to be supervising the children. Take notes, folks: life is not like school—it gives the test first and the lesson second. Think about it as you read about things that may never have crossed your minds regarding our schools and the bullying that occurs in them.

3

The Hallways

If you teach, did your principal ever tell you to try to be standing in the hallway near your classroom when classes change? It's a great idea for a number of reasons. For one, you get to talk and interact in a less-than-serious way with students, and they are able to see you in a different light—always a good thing. The second reason is that your mere presence can be a deterrent to inappropriate pushing, shoving, running, loud talking, etc., and therefore helps to keep some semblance of order in what for some kids is a very scary adventure—that of simply making a class change as they navigate the shark-infested waters of a typical school.

Yes, the scariest place in the school for young people is the hallways. On a regular basis, bullied children are given "flat tires," which occur when someone steps on your heel and makes your shoe come off. Books are knocked out of people's hands; hair is pulled; and racial epithets, slurs, and threats are made—soto voce, in small written notes, or sometimes out loud for all to hear. "Kick me" signs are old school—you can see them in the movie *Back to the Future*.

But they keep showing up with their retro appeal. Students are regularly touched and groped inappropriately, and even sucker-punched and propositioned. Often it happens instantaneously, mere feet from an adult supervisor in the hallway. When the punched student winds up in a heap on the floor, no one says a word as they keep walking—in the manner of citizens on a city street when violence happens right in front of them.

One black college student of mine said that his black friends would, on a specific day, sucker-punch several unsuspecting "nerdy white kids" just to see how many one-punch "knockouts" they could achieve in a marking period. Once, a boy in my school thought it would be funny to pull the wig off a girl having cancer treatments. It happened in the hallway near where three teachers were pretending to supervise. No one reported it till the mother of the girl called me that evening to ask me what I was going to do about this. The boy thought he was being funny. He did it right in the hallway, with crowds milling around. It wasn't a nice phone call. "How can you allow this kind of behavior to occur in your school, Mr. Principal?" Wait till you second-career people who decide to get certified in Educational Leadership get that question!

The Omerta, or code of silence, observed by students in most public—yes, *and* private—schools would make organized crime members envious. The hapless student who was punched looks around and sees no one looking at him in the role of attacker. He then reports it to a nearby teacher, who shrugs and says he can't help the student without some proof or witnesses. When the child tells his parents, the parents come storming in to confront the principal, who can provide not a shred of satisfaction. The school cameras provide a poor-quality image made less clear by light reflection anyway—school security cameras are always the cheapest ones that can be found in the catalogue—so everything is a silhouette at best! Insults of a racial, ethnic, sexual, or disability-related nature are passed back and forth all day long; and regardless of how alert the adults are, they are never seen or heard.

As stated previously, the media likes to write about cyberbullying—something the school can do nothing about, but things are being whispered in your child's ear or stated openly right in the middle of the hallway every class change, causing great trauma for children and causing them, for example, to be late for class as they take the long way around to avoid a bully or a certain group of bullies. In such a predatory zeitgeist, merely going to school at all quickly loses its appeal. This is exacerbated if a child looks different in some way—whether that be in terms of mode of dressing, hairstyle, skin color, gender, body shape, disability, etc. The child forced to take the long way is, of course, often late to class; and when questioned by a teacher with no discernment skills, he or she offers some lame excuse because more abuse will occur if the student names the perpetrators who are really causing the tardiness.

The often-undiscerning teacher chooses to make an example of this helpless individual, sending him or her to the office, where the student sits once again for the entire period and get denied the education they are supposed to be receiving because he or she is now at three absences or some aforementioned number at which the boom is lowered on the student. The vice principal knows the child and, although undiscerning about the bullying, often goes easy on the child, sending the child to the next class with the admonition "I better not see you down here again, Freddie, or you are going to force me to have to do something more serious than just talking, you understand me?" End of intervention. No justice given yet again. The bullies are somewhere laughing about this and how easy it is to pick on unsuspecting individuals.

Other students who are perennial targets will try to get through the day without going to the bathroom because of the gauntlet they must face in that scary and smoky little room. No adult enjoys spending time in the school restroom, so normally, they avoid these hellholes. Extortion occurs regularly here, and woe to the individual who has more to do than simply urinate, as water is splashed on them, firecrackers are set off, books and heads are flushed in the toilet, etc.

Practical jokes, as we used to call them, are not joking matters when injury occurs to another person or fear is instilled in others. One school person reported that a ramp in the main hallway had vegetable oil placed on it just prior to the bell to change classes, and near mayhem ensued. Funny? Ask the parents of children who lost teeth or were trampled in the ensuing melee of students sliding all over the ramp and knocking people down.

As previously stated, current architectural trends for new schools give no a priori consideration for the human interactions that occur every minute of the day. All architects should have to attend a seminar as part of their professional licensing, where they must learn about day-to-day happenings inside a school building.

To illustrate, an architect showed us his plans for a new stadium one night at a school board meeting. The drawing was beautiful, and the architect clearly explained everything down to the broad jump and pole vault pits that would be on the sides of the 53-yard-wide football field. Anything wrong with that picture?

We had to explain to the architect, board, and superintendent that this was not a football stadium but a sports stadium and the soccer parents would desire night games and soccer needs at least 70 yards of width, not to mention the ever-present band, parents who would want band shows to be held in the stadium, and how we would not want children playing instruments to trip while stepping in sawdust pits on the side of the football field or upon pieces of plywood placed to cover the pits. Architects, you *don't* get it either, despite your brilliance! But we digress again.

This has been a mere sampling of the happenings in one of the school's most dreaded places. If your child is willing to speak to you openly about these things, he or she will have much more to share about this recurring nightmare of hall passage than can be enumerated here. Teachers, look at the kid who is always late to class. Use some discernment. Is he really trying to beat the system, or is he more of a victim and is always late because he or she is taking the long way, even though it is never the kid's real excuse? Come on, teachers, you are better judges of character than that. Stop being so darn "write 'em up" happy! It's easy to come down hard on perennially targeted children; they don't talk back to you! Plus, it makes you look so darn tough!

We move now to the next most dreaded place in the school—the cafeteria.

4

The Cafeteria

Every school has children who like to spend their lunchtime helping the librarian or perhaps another teacher doing unspecified tasks. The motivation is not always altruistic. The simple truth is that many students would much rather be somewhere else than the scary cafeteria, where they are getting abused. One study of middle school bullying revealed that 83% of the surveyed population of eighth-grade students stated that they regularly see bullying in the cafeteria, followed by 77% reporting it in the classroom and other places with lower percentages. The average adult might walk into the same cafeteria and state that everything looks in order. After all, there are never any food fights!

Let's look at a typical cafeteria. The first thing you notice about lunchtime in, for example, a middle school, is that students (particularly boys up through about ninth grade) run to the cafeteria as though the cafeteria is about to run out of food or a prize is being given to whoever gets there first. It's not just a lack of maturity for many of these kids. Getting there ahead of the problem is more often the motivation than one's hunger and excitement about the cuisine—a fact of which you the reader are obviously aware!

This is because for too many years, the thinkers behind school lunches did not realize that at lunch, most individuals want something that looks like lunch as opposed to meat loaf and mashed potatoes or chicken pot pie and green beans almondine, which, though arguably good for you, will never look enough like the usual midday meal real people eat! What adult would eat mashed potatoes, celery with peanut butter, or garden-fresh peas at lunch? You would take McDonald's any day of the week, and Panera does not serve meat loaf. So the cuisine is not what causes the running through the halls. Beating the bad guys to the cafeteria is the focus.

The running, of course, causes pushing and shoving, flat tires, tripping, and books being knocked out of students' hands. Rather than wasting time going to a locker, a child will place his or her books in some book racks outside the cafeteria, which often become fair game for another student to, for example, place a piece of pizza in the middle of one's brand-new social studies book.

Another aspect of the pushing and shoving is that the students always arrive in the cafeteria ahead of the teachers who have duty because they are going to the bathroom and generally are in no big hurry to take on this dreaded responsibility each day. They will get there by and by—three to five minutes after the students. Maybe they have to stop at their mailbox first and kill some time talking intelligently with another actual adult in the office or making a quick phone call.

Butting in line is also a regular occurrence, but bullying has not started yet, because even the bullies have food on their minds at this point. However, as students stand in line, they are, on a regular basis, threatened—e.g., "If you give me some money, I'll be your friend." Or "If you don't give me some money, you are dead." (Not an actual death threat—it's just how kids talk—but the person being asked for money is clearly in trouble, and the adult does not even see or hear it).

Additionally, kids are pinched, fondled, propositioned, and hit; and it all goes unseen amid the general confusion and nonspecific orders from the cafeteria supervisors who are yelling things like, "Keep it down, you people!" "No butting!" "Wait your turn, boys!" All of which sound as though there is law and order, just no actual justice to the victim. The cafeteria ladies are often unhappy, and act like it is their own food they are parting with when a child has no money because it was just taken by a bully. ("Serves him right. He's years old now. He should remember his lunch or his money. Going hungry will teach him a good lesson, by God!") Or the student has had his lunch taken and receives a grudging peanut butter and jelly sandwich from one of these grumpy people—the plan B lunch in most places when a child "forgot" his money—again! At least it was before the sudden rash of peanut allergies. Ladies, please look at this child: do you think he is trying to beat you for a free lunch that will only be peanut butter and jelly? Seriously? I have one word for you: *discernment*! And it's not your peanut butter. It comes from the government, and is often free— for now at least, until politicians on one particular side of the political spectrum, eager to look financially prudent, cut the peanut butter and the free breakfasts.

The person supervising the lunch period is doing so in a legal sense only. Most people, as we stated, find the job distasteful, and one gets such a job more frequently if they happen to be big and loud. Petite and sweet young things don't get lunch duty. This goes to the meaner, nastier large people—the football coach, for example. The supervisors are not looking for "mismatches" in the line. This means identifying in advance who the likely assailants and victims will be and how, strangely enough, they always seem to be near each other in the line. For them, quiet and a straight line are much more desirable than justice because the latter requires actual thought and proactive planning. "Keep it down, people ,and keep that line straight. No pushing, boys!" Really, it sounds tough coming from the football coach even though it has no real value in terms of justice for the victim.

Next, the students are now eating the food, and it is always being thrown in the cafeteria, and it is virtually impossible to detect where it is coming from. Generally, the food gets thrown at the same people who like to sit at the same tables each day. Desserts are squished, food is taken with the warning that "you are dead if you tell anybody!" And if a student has to get up from the table to go to the bathroom, his food is always tampered with when he is gone. Principals pray that an inadvertent fire alarm caused by a dirty smoke head—they are seldom cleaned—does not go off during the lunches due to the number of student lunches that are tampered with, because justice is impossible to achieve because no one will be caught fooling with the food. Often, the bullies set someone up by throwing food and then all pointing to the innocent bullied individual, swearing that he or she did it; and the supervisor, rather than discerning whether such a person would actually commit such an offense in the first place, gullibly sends the student to the office to eat his or her lunch, to the delight of the bullies who have just done the exact same thing for the tenth day in a row—undiscerned, of course, by the big, tough person on duty.

We suspect that you think that this must be a concocted story, so we will share two such experiences with you from our own schooldays. In the first setting, all of us are in the auditorium for Foreign Language Night, listening to exchange students from area schools, including our own, talk about their American experiences. The presentations are boring, that's true, but I am doing my level best to appear interested because in my role as student council president, I have to look interested. My friends start making too much noise, in my opinion, so I get up in an effort to change my seat, because I think it might be a good idea to separate myself from my noisy friends—something, sadly, that should have occurred to me earlier. As I stand up to leave, a friend yells very loudly, "This garbage is boring. I'm leaving!" Everyone in the auditorium is now looking at me. Guess how that story ends? Imagine standing there naked trying to explain to no one in particular, nonverbally, that "it was not me" and later to the principal, who was, of course, "shocked and appalled" at *my* obnoxious behavior.

Shocked always seems to come with *appalled*, doesn't it? A funny practical joke? Let's get something straight: most practical jokes are done by people who are downright mean and nasty individuals trying to be entertained by the awkwardness of their victims. They do it because of how easy it is—like shooting the proverbial fish in a barrel. What about all the foreign exchange students who worked hard on their presentations and were getting laughed at? What about all the visitors and the unkind things they would be saying about the school in general, including the local education beat writer for the local newspaper? How could the Student Council president be so rude?

Here's a second example: Every morning, we had band practice for an hour. Almost every morning, an overweight Japanese American student whom we named Benny, a tuba player, was thrown out of rehearsal. Why? Because the band director, a willing dupe to our bullying pranks, thought that Benny was farting out loud. Every morning, one of us in the trumpet or trombone section would make a loud farting noise and then all get up yelling, "Yuck, gross! Come on, Benny, do you have to do that here? God, what a terrible smell!" Adults are such easy marks! I know, because like you, I wasn't always an adult!

Teachers on duty generally have their brain on Power Save and are wonderful dupes who will take the bait every time without grasping what is happening—and that is for the ones who are actually paying attention and not looking at their phones or talking with another adult. Again, no justice for the victim. Obviously, all of this is much worse for potential victims on days when a substitute teacher is present. When the sub is present and trouble is caused, and the sub asks, "What is your name, young man?," "Joe Smith" is often the answer; and subs are in school a lot—often on Mondays, Fridays, or as we get near to Christmas and people have gifts to wrap, for example.

Strangely, all of this bullying can happen with a monitor being a mere five feet away. Imagine you are on lunch duty. A child tells you that his food was taken again by a certain student. You ask that student where the food is. The answer to a question about what happened to the food is, "I don't know, I did not do it." Now what do you say? If you do not know the perpetrator, his reply when you ask his name may be "Joe Smith" again, so that won't help. The only thing you have to offer at this point is some muted generalized statement like, "If I even hear a word about you taking food again, you can go to the office and tell the principal why it wasn't you, do you understand me?" To the student, you just said "Wanh-wanh-wanh" in another language that they shake their heads at affirmatively. Later, they are probably laughing raucously.

Ralphie in the the famous TV movie *The Christmas Story* says, "Adults always say that when his teacher asks, 'Aren't some of you ashamed?' but we kids knew better." Ralphie was in third grade in that movie, I think, so kids learn this stuff early, folks. They know if you adults are *really* paying attention or just appearing to pay attention! In the absence of proof and the fact that a monitor cannot conduct an inquisition each time food is taken, the kid who loses the food usually just puts up with the abuse rather than tell you and get the usual official-sounding, justice-devoid "Wanh-wanh wanh" warning, and possibly another beating lately for being a squealer.

As for the concept of discernment, let's pretend that there are five kids in the lunch line. Their names are Mike Tyson, John McCain, Richard Cheney, Dick Butkus, and Richard Simmons. You know them all well. Mike comes up and says that Simmons just took his lunch money. Can we all pay a bit more attention to the characters? Is Simmons really going to take Tyson's money? Write the word down:

D-I-S-C-E-R-N-M-E-N-T. It was probably one of the other model students.

Sometimes the monitor's less-than-motivated approach is to make the entire table stay after to clean the cafeteria for a day, a week, etc. Once again, this does not bring any succor to the abused and bullied child. Things will continue as before, or maybe even get worse for the child because of the nonspecific action to punish the bad guys. The custodian is then unfairly burdened with these kids since the teacher is not going to stay to supervise the cleanup. The bullies can outsmart the monitors any day of the week. In the cafeteria, they know how to create distractions by making an apparent fuss in one place that distracts the monitor who then turns his or her back on the place where the real injustice is occurring. Watch *Back to the Future* next time when Biff and Marty are about to go at it in the cafeteria as the over-the-top crazy bald-headed principal/ captain of the aircraft carrier in the movie *Top Gun* is standing there. A paper airplane flies by and the principal is distracted, heading off to the new perpetrator! Sorry, Newt Gingrich, but having kids clean the school with the janitor makes for a huge liability problem.

Additionally, the cafeteria ladies usually practice nonselective supervision as well and tend to operate by the strategy that if you yell loud enough and often enough, the troops will shape up. If the cafeteria is too noisy, their opinion is always that "things would be better if these damn teachers who are off three months in the summer would just kick a little more butt!" If you will excuse the stereotype, it always seems that those who did not choose to go to college or older folks always think that the schools would be fine if a lot more butts were being kicked. Can you say lawsuit? How about child abuser? Those things happened less in the "good old days," folks. School districts in some states still hand out forms requiring parental permission to use corporal punishment, and the law in many of those same states also puts adults who hit children on a child abuser list. People, kicking *more* butts is not the answer. The kids are copying you by kicking plenty of butts—emotionally, at least—right under your noses!

Again, however, it's the same recurring theme: the victim's plight goes unaddressed. How hard is it to guess why the librarian always has a lot of "helpers" at lunchtime? Now we will go to another scary place in the building—the gym.

5

The Gym

In this context, when we say gym, we refer to the locker room, the actual gym, as well as the outside facilities for physical education. Without a doubt, the gym is a nightmare of epic proportions for young people. Let's begin with cell phones, which nobody is supposed to have with them in the gym according to the district policy manual but which everyone carries anyway. Since all phones now have a camera better than your regular camera at home with umpteen megapixels—picture several boys approaching one of the girls and paying her money to take a picture of a girl in the locker room. The picture goes viral, and all hell breaks loose. How does a school stop that kind of brutality? The answer is that they can't. The students have provided the solution: After elementary school, a growing number of children all the way up till their senior year choose not to dress for gym, take their F grade, and then go bowling for two weeks in the summer and write a report about it to get their PE credit. But the photo matter is the extreme. Let's talk about the normal day-to-day happenings. Students have things stolen from their lockers every day.

There are typically no windows in the locker room (those brilliant architects again), and now and then, someone turns the lights off, causing stygian darkness as students are punched, kicked, spat upon, and have their things disappear. Teachers are never walking around the locker room during the time provided for students to undress and dress. They have things to do in their office, or they must be in the gym because the school thought it was neat to put in a climbing wall for "lifetime sports" that no one uses but must now be constantly monitored so that no one climbs it without the proper harnessing device, which the school does not have—and there are no trained people to teach it anyway. Also, the locker room is invariably left open to the outside hallway (it's against the fire code to lock panic bar doors), and any student in a physical education class who wants to steal something or damage someone's property simply has to say that he or she needs to use the lavatory. Ask your child: few, if any, of them actually lock their gym lockers and they regularly leave valuables in their pants pockets or book bags.

Now the class starts and the exercises the students may be required to do place a student in a position to be ridiculed should they happen to be particularly uncoordinated or overweight. Happily, we aren't—for the most part— senselessly climbing ropes in gym class anymore, and would someone please tell me why we are still having students do pull-ups? What disease is this a cure for?

A basketball lesson begins, and while the teacher is looking the other way, a ball is thrown at someone's head—or the teacher's head. Has it occurred to anyone that real basketball is pointless in high school gym class because if the student has no basketball skills by that time, who cares? Make the class fun and participatory with activities where it is hard to embarrass oneself. Wedgies are regularly meted out in PE class, shorts are pulled down, and for obvious reasons, nobody actually gets a shower anymore. Ask your parents or grandparents about their harrowing tales from the days of taking showers in gym class. For the most part, towels are not being snapped anymore, but the Marine Physical Fitness Test is still being administered, which contains things that will guarantee that the average student is placed in an embarrassing situation and made the object of ridicule. *But we need to toughen these kids up*, one of you is thinking. Really? Why? So the kids can tolerate the abuse easier? Come on, folks! That is not the aim of building resiliency—so one can better tolerate the miscreants! Besides, the military trains its own. Fitness for defense of the nation is no longer the role of physical educators.

Writing about the locker room of a middle school, Ben Montgomery of the *St. Petersburg Times* offered the following:

> The Boy's Locker Room is one of the scariest places in America, a minefield of adolescence where danger lurks behind every shower stall and plastic soap dispenser. It is also a place where teen tomfoolery advances to hazing and bullying and animalistic brutality. This was the case at a Florida middle school where prosecutors said when 4 teens raped another boy with a broom handle and a hockey stick.

We will spare you the details; use your imagination. In Pennsylvania, a fourteen-year-old boy held down a thirteen-year-old while others urinated on him. In Alabama, a twelve-year-old boy suffered serious burns when someone lit a can of aerosol deodorant that was being sprayed on him. Every one of you reading this book has a locker room story where you were the perpetrator, the victim, or the amused bystander who said nothing as the bullying (that you called a practical joke) was taking place under the teacher's nose.

In an article by Violet Hassler in the *Enid News*, a student named Lance described himself as not just the target of bullying in gym class but the "favored victim." "I am the official punching bag of gym class because kids think it is funny to come up and hit me, even when they are mad at someone else." Since Lance has trouble expressing himself, the teacher only adds to the difficulty by referring to Lance as "dumb" because of how unclear he is, which makes the teacher less able or willing to administer justice.

Particularly in middle school, children can become a convenient target who provides comic relief to the bullies and places a child's life in danger. Often, a situation such as this causes a parent to come see the principal and complain. The principal sends a memo to the teacher, and the teacher makes a general announcement—something like this: "If anybody touches _____again, heads are going to roll, people! Do you understand me?" The teacher, approaching the situation in the customary decontextualized manner by sounding tough once again fails to give the victim justice and will clearly add to the abuse the child is receiving behind the scenes, which will make the child less likely to report such a problem to any adult, including his parents, in the future.

One experienced female teacher that we know, after being told to do a better job of supervision in her locker room, put out this memo to all students: "The principal has directed me to tell you that he will be punishing people with greater severity if this current behavior continues…" Some teachers don't like to have to change the incompetent way in which they have been supervising, so memos like this come out so that they can still be "buds" with their students. The teachers' union will always come to the aid of these incompetent "professionals." How dare one tell them what they could be doing better?

The assessment methods of teachers may also still be in the dark ages, so a weaker student is exposed when everyone is watching the pull-ups, push-ups, ten left-handed layups, or cartwheels being attempted for a grade. This serves as a motivator for the bullies who pick up where the assessment leaves off. Students are still receiving award for things in physical education based on the physical gifts they entered the class with as opposed to the ones acquired in class. Thus a significant improvement in a long-distance run by an overweight child, for example, might go unnoticed as the A grade goes to the child who was fast to begin with but made no actual improvement during the semester, since physiologically, one cannot make significant improvement in much of anything anatomically in only two PE periods a week. This encourages disparaging comments, fat jokes, and other forms of abuse that will stay with that child for years. PE teachers, check class attendance or medical excuse patterns—they will always increase when an activity that exposes one's physical inadequacies is taking place. Could it be that tenth-grade girls really do not need to learn how to punt a football or head a soccer ball? Who is writing this curriculum? Shuttle run? Softball throw? Please! Let's just have fun and do some sweating in the process. Physical education is not the minor leagues for the varsity sport teams. The varsity coaches already have their lineups picked out before the season starts. The biggest lie in coaching—as all coaches will tell you—is when, on the first day of practice, the coach tells the players that all the jobs are wide open!

To Mrs. Obama, your efforts at combating childhood obesity are commendable, but having kids doing jumping jacks on the White House lawn? Jumping jacks are on page 1 of the exercise book, copyright 1952! Could one of your non-jock aides have done just two to three minutes more of research and come up with something that's fun and causes the same physiological effect as the jumping jacks? Does the First Lady really think that kids can't wait to get home and do jumping jacks? There I go digressing again!

Again, all of this is merely an overview. Teachers can get into a routine where they become blind to the actions they take that help to foster more bullying rather than less. The dread of choosing teams in class is something many grownups still have nightmares about. The simple action of picking captains, drafting players, or having to be in a relay race (Groan…Oh no! We have John on our team! We are doomed!") helps to instigate greater abuse for young people who are, for example, always picked last. This is the first mention we have made about teacher praxis and how it can be something that adds to a bullied student's woes. Next we move to the regular classroom where unaware adults are a leading cause of bullying owing frequently to defective praxis.

6

The Classroom

Picture this scenario. You are a victim of bullies who happen to be in the same class with you. Every time the teacher turns his or her back, the bully hits you, or bumps your arm, or wrinkles your paper. Finally, you retaliate by whacking the bully just as the teacher turns around and sees you doing it. The bully feigns bloody murder, like in the example of your little brother in the beginning of this book, and you wind up with in-school suspension as the teacher ships you to the office, not willing to hear your tale of woe. The bully, being better at this criminal activity, knew how to pick his spots, while you did not. This goes on all the time. Many teachers, as we mentioned previously, make a big production out of student's tardiness, yet many of those same teachers never analyze (1) who is being late all the time (2) whether or not this child is someone who might be trying to beat the system, and (3) whether this student looks more like a victim or a bully.

Usually, you can tell with great accuracy, although girls can fool a teacher—especially a male teacher—much better than boys. How many teachers pay attention to seating arrangements? Where are the potential troublemakers in relation to the students likely to be bullied? Students with autism spectrum disorder are big targets of the bullies because of their particular thinking patterns, honesty, and, often, gullibility.

The politicians think that education would be greatly improved if we just had more geniuses doing the teaching and packing heat along with it. They never mention pedagogical skills as a prerequisite, thus making you, the parents, and the general public think that anyone can be a teacher as long as they are brilliant in algebra, for example, or were once a chemist, or a musician. Or a captain in the Marine Corps.

When I started a job in mid–school year as a principal in a demographically multicultural suburban high school in Philadelphia, I decided to take a walk around on my first day and see what goes on in this big building. Off in the distance, I thought I heard what sounded like screaming. I kept telling myself that this couldn't be real screaming by someone, but perhaps someone was showing a movie with the volume turned up too loud. I followed the sound and decided to watch, inconspicuously, what was happening through a window. The physics teacher was a person hired during the great push for hiring brilliant people instead of actual teachers with pedagogical skills. This nice man had a brilliant career in physics in the defense industry and was a graduate of MIT! I found myself fascinated as I watched an AP Physics class. Now, we know that anyone taking physics is usually very motivated and does not misbehave or try to disrupt the class. As it turned out, the students were all happily talking, reading, and generally seemed unaware of the teacher, and the teacher simply kept getting louder over the year, until he was actually yelling over the din created by the loud students. Nobody was angry, and the students were acting in a carefree manner while the teacher droned on about something about electrical currents. Occasionally, the teacher would say, "Now come on, people, quiet down, because this will be on the exam, so I want to see you taking good notes…" And so it went, with me in shock as I watched this physics lesson being taught by a person literally screaming close to the top of his lungs to a class full of seemingly content talkative young people.

What is the point? The point is that many teachers lack simple pedagogical skills that maintain order before the incident occurs. If anything, the classroom is the one place in the school where an alert teacher that keeps students engaged can prevent any type of bullying behavior. Compare this to the supervisory requirements of, say, the school bus driver who is told to supervise students by putting his or her back to them! Not a job for the faint of heart.

My old sixth-grade teacher, for example, could write on the chalkboard with either hand and still look at the class. It would have been hard to sneak in a punch with good old

Mrs. Smiley in charge. When teachers go up or down an outside row to check student work, is that desk *against* the wall? If it is against the wall, the teacher must turn his or her back to the class to look at the student's work. If the desks are away from the wall, then the teacher walks down the outside row *next* to the wall, which means when he or she looks at the student work, they are *still* facing the class instead of away from the class!

Wow, how simple. I bet that you brilliant businessmen and scientists and elected officials and media folks out there who think anybody can teach never thought about that, did you? How about the way a teacher praises students? If a teacher in a middle school says, "John, you did such a brilliant job on the test. Too bad some of your classmates aren't as serious as you are. Thank you, John. Well done!" Poor John might get pounded rather than complimented by his peers when he gets out in the hallway.

Returning to the issue of being on time for class: do you remember the teacher who would ask, "Why are you always late?" to a student who would not have an answer and would wind up getting punished? That student is usually a targeted individual, not a perpetrator of violence. He was late to avoid the bad guys again.

Many schools have a wooden board with the room number on it or some more formal sign-in and sign-out process for the use of the lavatory. Teachers, have you looked closely at who is going out and the time they are always asking to leave the room?

Imagine that pedagogical skills are like golf clubs in a golf bag. The rules of golf state that a person may have up to fourteen clubs in his or her bag. How many of you had that teacher or coach who only had a driver in his or her bag and handled every situation in the same booming way? Sometimes a wedge, or a putter is all that is needed to correct a problem. A teacher with pedagogical skills takes the time to size up a situation and carefully selects the next club to do the job. Brilliant people have no training in pedagogy, and this lack of training is something that every self-respecting bully figures out in a single day. That is why many teachers, like our old band director who always kicked poor Benny out of band practice despite his innocence, are such an easy touch for a bully. Yes, media and politicians, lack of education is crucial to a successful education for our children, but the expertise that is needed is not in the subject area, but in the area of pedagogy—teaching skills, that is.

Here is a true story. In my eighth-grade U.S. history class, we would witness a girl who had had the misfortune of developing too early get fondled regularly in class by two boys while the teacher—a woman perhaps seventy-five years of age—never saw it. What was the poor girl to do, complain about it in class? The teacher refused to change anyone's seats "till the next marking period," and she was always writing all her notes on the chalkboard with her back turned, and the routine never changed. Along with the outrageous behavior of the two boys, spitballs were thrown at other students and George Washington's portrait by Gilbert Stuart which, by January, was encrusted with dried spitballs. Papers were being crumpled, and the teacher's usual reaction—completely devoid of justice was generally that if she heard another "peep" out of any of us, we'd all have more homework; and of course, when she turned her back on us, someone always said the word *peep*, which gave us yet more homework.

Of course, back then, the prevailing zeitgeist was, "Boys will be red-blooded American boys, and girls love the attention anyway, and it's just practical jokes. These kids aren't robbing banks, for heaven's sake!" Does anyone think these things no longer exist? Ask the bullies.

There is always a TV show where an ex-con is evaluating someone's home for its lack of safety features. People should bring a bully along as they walk through a school. Ask the bully how the expensive programs about bullying that the district are having so they can brag about how proactive they are being are working.

A well-trained teacher can eliminate all bullying in the classroom. That is when the teacher is at his or her cognitive sharpest. Unhappily, many colleges who prepare aspiring teachers are manned by people who spent a year or two in a real school, saw how unruly things can be, and scampered off to the safety of a university, where they get to write about how to deal with bullying—from a safe distance.

7

The School Bus

School architecture up to the last few years never included lanes for all the cars driven by parents each day that drop off and pick up children and drive the administration crazy. High school students and the parents of younger children try to avoid the school bus at all costs: "I'm not letting my child sit among the great unwashed" might be your attitude. For many high school students, it's an embarrassment to say that one must ride the bus each day. Whatever the reason, the school buses are their own separate gauntlet that a child faces each day, and the problem is even greater in school districts with a large amount of square miles, because in these geographically large districts, there is only one bus run, and all the schools start at the same time— thus, the kindergarten child has to ride the bus with high school seniors. The high school principal is always being called in these big geographical districts by the mother of the kindergarten kid who is learning new words from the high school kids that Mom and Dad do not appreciate hearing at the dinner table—assuming, of course, anyone is still sitting down to dinner in this era. A quaint notion, to be sure!

Students are typically under less supervision coming and going to school than at any time during the school day. With their attention properly diverted to the road, bus drivers have an amazingly limited capacity for attending to the children and often only react when there is too much noise. Additionally, every filled school bus has more students in it than the average classroom where the teacher spends most of the time looking at the students, and for which, school administrators quickly find a substitute or coverage if the teacher will not be present. One survey of bus drivers revealed that, in their collective opinions, only 5% of the children cause problems on the bus. (We would correct this to say *visible* problems). However, the action of one person could result in a terrible tragedy for all the passengers.

Are parents overprotective because they all drive their children to school and pick them up each day? Tell it to the parents of Christopher Gonzalez, for example, a five-year-old who was pushed out the emergency door of a moving bus as it rounded a corner, fracturing his skull. The child had been bullied repeatedly up to the time of the incident, and the bus driver, like many adults, just thought it was kids being kids with some of the usual horseplay, all the while not even realizing that the child was no longer on the bus! A mother of an elementary child in Western, Pennsylvania, reported that her child's hearing aids were ripped out of her child's ears and thrown out the bus window, with the driver being completely unaware.

Also, very few school districts have their own buses anymore. This means that there is very little hope of consistent discipline—if any—being applied in the school buses because the driver is not beholden to school officials in any way, except when he or she, completely bereft of management tools, parks the bus by the side of the road and refuses to move the bus until an administrator comes out and kicks some butt for a change. Bus drivers tend to think like the cafeteria ladies when it comes to kicking more butt…the country would be so much better, by God!

In some of the more remote school districts, a person leasing as few as two or three buses gets the same opportunity to contract with the school district for transportation as the company with an entire fleet of buses. That usually means that people with limited education and experience with supervision of children who are free to work part-time are your bus drivers—at a tasteful $10 per hour with no benefits. As stated above, these often-nice folks generally think that all the school problems could be solved if the people in charge would kick a little more butt. Thus a child may fear riding the bus because of a crazy bus driver. We recall one situation where a bus driver blared a radio with Christian music during the entire bus run, and when asked to at least turn it down, became indignant, referring to us as anti-Christian! Another bus driver would curse and swear regularly at the children who, of course, are experts at getting an untrained adult to take the bait and lose their temper as we spoke about with our band director example. When this occurs, the bus driver usually stops the bus somewhere and refuses to drive any farther till an administrator comes out and punishes "*all* of them!"

The law asserts that the school is responsible for each student who is transported to school from the time they leave their house in the morning till they return. That notion sounds great, but is essentially ridiculous because school personnel have enough to worry about in the building, and believe it or not, school administrators are not really like the assistant principal in the movie *Ferris Bueller's Day Off*, with the time to follow errant students around town all day like idiots or assuming responsibility for what happens on their street. That being said, the bullies are hard at work early in the morning at the bus stop, late in the afternoon, and on the ride itself to and from school. That is why traffic patterns have changed drastically at all schools, as most parents would rather pick up and drop off their child, and the original designs of parking lots have been revised because the architects did not know about bullying. Overprotective? Tell it to the parents of children undergoing this terror every day. Additionally, even the students who are not bothered have learned early on to keep their mouths shut, lest they be next on the hit list of the bullies.

Kids are regularly hit; kicked; spat upon; groped; verbally assaulted; propositioned; "borrowed" money from having their musical instruments, books, and other belongings tampered with; denied seats; tripped—the abuse, is, quite simply, endless. Occasionally, we see a story in the news about a parent who, fed up with a school's seeming inaction, takes matters into their own hands—like Madea in the movie—and goes on to a school bus to verbally and/or physically confront the bullies.

Interestingly, the one place where significant efforts have been made to improve the proactive management skills of staff, perhaps more than any other segment of employees related to the schools, is the training that bus drivers are receiving in many places in this country.

Transportation directors around the country, working with the school administrative staff, have been taking a variety of proactive measures to eliminate the incidences of bullying on their buses with specialized training for their drivers. Unfortunately, in the schools of education around the country as well as the in-service programs for teachers in school districts where test scores are the priority, very little time is dedicated to providing the teaching staff with strategies necessary to confront bullying in the places in which they work. Beyond "big and mean-looking," there is no effort at bringing in experts from the field of police science, for example. In the schools, we suffer from decontextualized supervision. That is no longer the case with school bus companies. Transportation supervisors are starting to "get it" as prevention programs have become decidedly proactive rather than reactive, with some very positive results. For example, Jeff Porter, a Michigan Transportation supervisor asserts that his district has taken steps to "bully-proof" itself.

In specialized training, the staff was taught about the various kinds of bullying, learned *what* to look for in terms of student behavior that might provide clues in advance regarding a victim or a bully (contextualize supervision!), and all adults were familiarized with bullying prevention tactics. Jim Ellis, a transportation director in New York State, asks drivers to be cognizant of what he refers to as "target kids" (again, supervision with context!)—ones that seem likely to be victims. Drivers are then encouraged to make certain that a safe environment is provided for these students. In Orange County, California, Ellen Johnson, transportation supervisor, asserts that adults are trained to be good listeners and to take the comments of students seriously. Also, the staff has been taught the importance of maintaining confidentiality, which serves to discourage retaliation against the bullied victims and keeps the "kid grapevine" viable, with students always ready to come forward in the manner of the police who cultivate their underworld sources. Drivers are also instructed to watch for signs that signify that a student might be a victim of bullying. This can include, for example, shyness, insecurity, cautious behavior, and lateness to the bus. Continuing with a theme of being proactive, Mark Obtinario of Castle Rock, Washington, emphasizes techniques for all school personnel such as behavior management training with increased administrative support combined with a mentoring program for drivers. Indeed, in many places, students confide more readily with an unlettered but caring bus driver rather than with the guidance counselor who wants all involved to sit around a table and "talk it out."

Often, in a school district, there are good bus routes and bad bus routes, depending on what part of town the bus travels to pick up and drop off students. Many transportation contractors operate by seniority with the experienced bus drivers picking the good routes and the rookies being assigned the other ones.

Michael Dorn is executive director of Safe Havens International who has encouraged school bus drivers to pay close attention to the demeanor of students. Things like facial expression, composure, and body language can speak volumes when one knows what to look for and can provide context to the supervisory practices of the adults during the school day. Many school districts state that there are cameras on the buses, but the real truth is that not all the cameras have film in them. The cameras that actually work are usually moved around to various buses and, since they are mounted in the front of the bus, provide a very grainy image, often making it impossible to see who the perpetrators are. We admit to a moment of perverse glee when a parent stormed into the office one day claiming her child was being bullied, how she was suing the district, and how her child "never lies to me." We plopped the video into the TV and pushed the button. You should have seen Mom's face as her daughter was featured in the video as the lead perpetrator in a bullying episode!

One paradigm shift might greatly improve the situation with bullying on the school bus. Dr. Ellen de Lara of Syracuse University posits that the bus ride must be viewed as an integral part of the student's school day and school experience. She wants school administrators to become more aware of the problems that the drivers are facing, arguing that the administrators cannot just view the bus ride as something other than a part of the school day. Administrators expend a lot of time and effort to ensure a safe and scholarly environment inside the building, yet a school bus has more students than a classroom, and the adult nominally in charge must place his or her back to the riders. A place the size of a bus with sixty kids would never go without as many as two supervisors were that group in the building. Clearly, there should be an adult who sits in the back seat of every bus looking forward. Bullies won't sit in the back of a bus where an adult occupies the back seat! No school district or bus company would pay for such a thing, however.

One cannot help but be encouraged by the proactive approach taken by transportation directors. An adult sitting in the back would make that part of the bus significantly less desirable for the bad guys.

Here's the news, all of you mental health professionals: this is real stuff—nothing is made up here—and riding the bus is torture every day for children who have usually learned long ago that they might as well not talk about it, because they will get even more abuse. Once again, nothing noticeable happens with the adult nearby, yet a girl could be having something inappropriate whispered in her ear, or a kid could be getting touched in some inappropriate manner, or perhaps their expensive violin is being damaged, and no adult can see it; and no kid—not even the victim— dares to talk about it.

We are betting you think that all of this is exaggerated. Really, it can't be that bad, can it? At least it can't happen in my upper middle-class community where the people fancy their schools to be like private schools having the benefit of de facto segregation. Students from well-to-do backgrounds, in our experience, are significantly more heartless and cruel than some of their lower socioeconomic counterparts. Generally, they do not ride the bus, however. Their parents are available to transport them to and from school.

8

Bullying of Children with Special Needs

If you were the parent of a child with special needs, you might be angry—at the world in general. The anti-bullying alliance posits that having a disabled child can have a huge impact on family life—and we might add, this is when everything is simply going right. Parents, continues the alliance, face a unique combination of emotional, social, physical, and financial pressures that impact on family life. Parents of special needs children often feel alone and isolated. Now comes a situation where their child is being bullied either directly or in an indirect manner characterized by isolation, exclusion, or being the butt of what some still call a practical joke, and it is being done out in the open in most instances, with adults around.

In an online survey, one repeated theme was anger. These parents already have asked everyone, including God, *Why us?* They are trying diligently, as only a loving parent can, to help their child fit in, to be accepted as one of the group.

A report by the Archives of Pediatrics and Adolescent Medicine reported on by Michelle Diament from 2012 states, "Roughly half of adolescents with autism, intellectual disability, speech impairments and learning disabilities are bullied at school." We would argue that the percentage is higher, but there is no one truly accurate way to show this except by reports by children who have the intellectual capacity to articulate this without fear of further bullying.

One thing is sure, and that is that students with various disabilities since the early '70s are more likely than ever to be in a classroom with children who do not have disabilities. Under the Individuals with Disabilities Education Act (IDEA), students are guaranteed a Free and Appropriate Public Education (FAPE), and that means that efforts at mainstreaming students for some subjects during the school day have been successful. This exposure to students who do not have special needs are a guarantee that the acts of bullying will continue to increase. As we are writing this, an article appeared in the *Washington Post* describing a boy of sixteen in a local high school who is autistic. It seems he came into contact with two girls in his school—one who he still views as his girlfriend and her older friend. These girls made videos that became viral and caused great outrage. The girls are now facing criminal prosecution as adults for the things they did to this boy. They filmed themselves kicking him in the groin, asking him to recover a basketball that was on thin ice and the boy fell through the ice and almost drowned. Neither girl made any effort to assist this boy. When he finally got out, they put him in the trunk of their car to go home, lest he get the insides of the car "wet." All the while, they continued to drain his bank account, which his father finally discovered, and called the police. Another video shows the girls holding a knife to the boy's throat. By the way, we did tell you that the perpetrators were girls, right? This incredible cruelty goes on every day in every school in this country. By the way, these were "nice kids" from a "nice neighborhood."

Autistic children alone who are mainstreamed for many subjects are the biggest targets because they are out there with the students who do not have a disability. A frequent type of bullying that happens under the nose of adult supervisors is called the *set-up*. In the set-up, either to play a practical joke on a student with special needs or one of their friends, several students will prompt a special needs student—for example, one with autism—by telling him that a certain girl really likes him. So he should write her a note or bring her a gift, or give her a kiss. When the autistic student does what he was prompted to do, everyone enjoys the big joke—sometimes even the autistic child, who interprets all of this attention as meaning that these seemingly attentive students are his friends.

The other more serious issue occurs when the child with special needs is a female who is physically mature and perhaps in a middle school. Boys will do inappropriate and/or immoral things with this girl who may not be able to communicate the abuse. Sometimes, the abuse goes undiscovered, until the young lady becomes pregnant. Clearly, students with special needs are not hidden away in the boiler room, as in the '60s—nor should they be concealed—and they buy their lunch like the other kids and eat in the cafeteria. Thus, if they have good speaking ability, bullies will take their money by telling these children that they will be the special needs children's friends if they lent the bullies some money. Of course, children with special needs always think that the kids fooling with him are their friends. This is why the boy in the *Washington Post* story did not want to get these vicious girls in trouble—they had convinced him that they were his friends.

A 2012 study in published in the Archives of Pediatrics and Adolescent medicine asserts that autistic children who are mainstreamed are four times as likely to be bullied by their classmates. Often, their money is taken on the promise that the person asking for the money "will be their friend" if they can get the money.

Everyone grows up, and the time arrives during middle school where a boy with special needs will feel the same about girls as every other boy as the hormones begin their raging. However, when he tries to show it by perhaps writing a note to the young lady or giving her flowers, his social awkwardness and inability to read the situation clearly leads to a reaction like "Ewww, get away from me, you disgusting retard!" That is what I heard on one occasion as a middle school teacher as the rest of a group of girls laughed raucously at the boy's awkwardness. Empathy is often beyond the ability of, for example, a middle school child without special needs. Imagine that you are the parent of the young man who has these normal adolescent feelings: Do you scream, cry, laugh? It would make me feel like crying; then I would be back to pleading and trying to make a deal with God. Put yourself in their place if you are a school employee. Look up the word *empathy*.

The closest I ever came to losing it completely and going after a student when I was a high school principal was when a young man was caught pulling the wig off the head of a girl undergoing cancer treatments. It happened in a hallway intersection where three different teachers, ostensibly on duty, were talking and paying only slight attention. Everything seemed orderly to them. No one saw it happen. The bullies always know when to strike.

Students prey upon the less fortunate. As scary as it sounds, it is true. Students are always imitating other students with special needs—their physical impediments, their language impediments, such as stuttering or high-pitched voice, or their nervous, uncontrollable movements. Students doing this kind of imitation right in the hallways or classrooms are seldom made to answer for this disrespectful treatment of fellow classmates. Occasionally, imitations can be positive, however, such as where students having cancer treatments are left without hair and fellow classmates all cut their hair off. These touching acts of kindness are always on the evening news. Unfortunately, set-ups and imitations of a negative variety aren't sexy-enough stories to make it to the news. Students who act in this disrespectful way need to be given some community service time serving as peer assistants in special education classrooms. For many, it is eye-opening and a great way to foster empathy and to augment a positive student climate. More on this strategy and others in the final chapter.

Teachers who previously may not have had students with special needs being mainstreamed to such an extent need to turn up their observation skills a few notches. Besides, having multiple forms of assessment and options built into their syllabi for other pathways to an A grade, teachers need to assess the players, the setting, the task, and the interactions that occur in their classroom. The physical education teacher needs to have the mainstreamed child's locker close by to his office so he can observe the locker room interactions at a glance.

All of us have stories that may involve our unkind behavior toward those with disabilities. While we were never overt in our ill treatment of children with special needs when I was a high school student, I recall with great shame referring to a girl who had an extreme birth defect from thalidomide with a pronounced limp as Flipperafter the '60s TV program main character who is a trained seal because of the girl's deformed appendage.

Closer scrutiny on the part of the adults does not mean military precision and walking in single file with no talking; it means watching closely when certain children with special needs are passing through the hallway. What are their peers doing when the student with an exceptionality is near? Who are the characters on the stage? A little closer attention—contextualized attention—can make many incidences of this type of bullying disappear.

9

Girl vs. Girl Bullying

We are not stereotyping here when we assert that girls, typically, are different than boys when it comes to bullying. To begin with, in many instances, girls are more vicious than boys in their bullying tactics. A conversation with any school administrator charged with maintaining law and order in the school will reveal that, for example, ninth-grade girls are collectively the most vicious of all and often get involved in physical altercations that draw big crowds of students anxious to see a hair-pulling match. Often, girls in this age group will band together to physically attack another girl. They work in groups more so than boys, and will use proxies more often to engage their victims. Typically, boys of the same age stay far away from these girls, and it is not unusual for these girls to manipulate their mothers into the conflict to be their proxies while they sit back and enjoy the show that they helped to instigate—like Bugs Bunny in the cartoon who is standing by a tree eating a carrot and watching the fight he instigated, saying, "What's up, Doc?"

There have been many incidents nationwide where the mother of a middle school or high school girl, unhappy with the perceived inaction of the school administration—a perception that is more real than imagined, because it is harder for school officials to accept the fact that girls are as nasty as, and sometimes nastier than, boys—will come onto a school bus or meet the bullies on the street to take them head-on. Madea in the sitcom goes onto a school bus and whacks the assailant of one of her kids. These unfortunate situations always wind up with the parent being arrested for assault, and the bullies and the victims are required to sit down and accept counseling, which turns out far less effective as a solution to the bullying than the mental health professionals would like to have us believe. That is because it takes on a preconceived false equivalence that the two parties are equal warring factions and that this bullying problem would disappear "if everyone learned to get along like polite young ladies." Sadly, both the perpetrators and the bullies know better. They are laughing at you, so-called professionals.

In the United States, a number of support groups have been created in an effort to provide girls with the tools necessary to change their behaviors. Some of the names of these support groups include Owning Up, Girls Circle, the Ophelia Project, Salvaging Sisterhood, and Full Esteem Ahead. The stated purpose of these groups, which are sponsored by both schools and community/church organizations, is to help the girls realize that cliques have real or imagined destructive power and how the better idea is to learn how to form more positive and inclusive relationships with peers.

These all-powerful, highly judgmental cliques who whisper behind people's backs, look down their noses at those judged inferior to them, yet smile to the right adults can be found in every school and at every level. Grown men in the schools are especially easy touches for these narcissistic and nasty females

While still referred to as bullying, the new term being used about girl-to-girl interaction is *relational aggression* by the guidance counselors and mental health professionals. These terms sound like poetic euphemisms.

Strangely, most boys seem oblivious to these issues; but if you are a female, you understand what the following people are talking about when they use the term *relational aggression*.

Rosalind Wiseman wrote the book *Queen Bees and Wannabees* on which the movie *Mean Girls* was based. In it, a ninth-grade girl feared for her life, and it began when she started receiving threatening text messages about being harmed physically if she dared to like a certain boy. Julia Taylor, an author and counselor, wrote about a young lady who was terrorized by a clique, and she always thought that the girls were her friends. This girl was allergic to peanuts, and her "friends" shoved crumpled-up peanut butter cookies in her face. The school administrators' response to the mother's complaint was a shocking "Oh, they were probably unaware of her allergy anyway!" Numerous girls have been abused for being either too well developed too early, or being called "flat as a board" for the reverse.

Girls get into physical violence, to be sure, but unlike boys, girl bullying tactics often involve groups and can be done in quiet ways, making it even less noticeable to those who employ decontextualized supervisory skills.

Mike Hardcastle, who provides advice for teens, points out some of the bullying tactics that girls are more likely to be of the emotional variety as opposed to the physical. Note how various tactics like these would not be readily observable unless someone had some advance warning so that he or she knew what they were looking for. The following would be typical examples of that type of bullying:

Anonymous prank phone calls or harassment from dummy e-mail accounts.

Playing jokes or tricks designed to maximize the victim's embarrassment with no apparent reason for the alienation.

Encouraging other children to ignore or pick on a specific child for no reason.

Inciting others to serve as proxies to act upon someone in a violent way.

Vandalizing the property or home of another girl.

Deliberate exclusion of others for no apparent reason.

Whispering in front of other kids with the intent to make them feel left out or *quiet targets*.

Name calling, rumor spreading, and other malicious verbal interactions.

Being friends one week and then turning against a peer the next week

Girls also tend to use alienation, ostracism, deliberate and calculated random exclusions, and spreading of rumors as bullying tactics because they are raised not to be physical in their dealing with others. Obviously, girls have physical confrontations, far more than in the "old days," but generally speaking, there remains a different level of physicality in the bullying tactics of girls versus boys. To the typical male adult, the actions of the girls are completely invisible. They are the rocks on the Star Trek planet, and the girls are the crew members from the starship. Men generally resort quickly to parental false equivalency when a problem occurs and simply say, "I want all of you to be quiet and get out of here, or everybody is getting suspended!" One of us was a principal in a high school, and we used this type of strategy because it was impossible to figure out who the perpetrator was—colleagues have all said that they employ the same generalized strategy to at least give the appearance of riding herd.

When one sees a group of girls in the hallway, for example, they could be bullying, and to the untrained eye, it may appear as though they are just standing around. Girls can be very predatory in their bullying, but the football coach on hall duty with the booming voice, or the assistant principal trying to make friendly small talk to develop some rapport, or the hall monitor might not categorize what they see as bullying, thus any subsequent disciplinary action that is meted out might be different—again, with both the perpetrators and the victims having to sit in a circle with the guidance counselor to discuss their differences. Once again, we have no justice for the victim.

On the other hand, if you were to ask adult females in the school, they know exactly what is going on with the girls because they lived it and were on one or both sides of this female style of bullying—particularly eighth to ninth-grade girls. There has been research where women in their seventies, when asked about the behavior of girls when they were in school, can remember the names of the bullies as if it were yesterday. Comprehending the emotional quagmire, they often chose to walk away from the problem, perhaps thinking, *The vice principal is just going to talk with them anyway.* Or, *The men will rationalize that it's 'typical girl-to-girl catfight' stuff anyway, and I am not getting involved in all of that!* Students, however, love the classic catfight and will encourage both warring factions during the day and not say a word in advance to an adult about the impending battle.

Galen and Underwood argue that teachers tend to ignore female-on-female violence, yet many students, as explained by Birkenshaw and Eslen, feel that social exclusion was the worst form of bullying. In the words of Suzanne SooHoo, one cannot address that which one chooses not to see.

Mike Hardcastle asserts that adults are often slow to react to girls who bully. He posits that when there is actual visible physical violence occurring, adults will usually be quick to intervene, but when the bullying takes on a less obvious form, even adults don't seem to know what to do, nor, we would add, do they know the settings in which this type of bullying is likely to start or where it is carried out. Since adults don't always label the tactics used by girls as bullying, kids who fall victim do not know where to turn for help.

Okay, so now, what? Having heard all of that, and realizing that even more blatant examples of bullying go virtually unseen by decontextualized supervisors, we realize that girl- to-girl bullying has even a smaller chance of being seen or accepted as a reality in this "good" school. The girls have lovely smiles. They can manipulate the toughest of adult male teachers/coaches/ administrators—at least to the point where an adult male will always be surprised when a really "nice" girl is identified as a ringleader of the bullying clique.

Whether girls are a part of a clique or not, all girls are affected because the behaviors spoken of, like alienation and exclusion, are going on all around them. Knowing the way the pecking order mentality works, explains GreatSchools, will teach the girls how they can rise above the problem and recognize it in themselves and others.

Technology greatly exacerbates the problem because children are never without their phones sending text and Twitter messages virtually around the clock. Also, it is far easier to be anonymous when communicating electronically. Julia Taylor asserts that lives can be ruined with one click of the phone!

Also, many parents, notably those women whose girls are important players in cliques, tend to downplay the problem by asserting that they went through the same things, and look, they did not turn out so bad, did they?

It is these girl-to-girl interactions that the adults try to fix with all parties sitting down and talking like friends with one another. It is one of the principal strategies used because a three-day suspension does not seem equitable to the three-day suspension given to a student for punching somebody. However, the victim once again is not given justice but treated like an equal participant in the aggressive and inappropriate actions that began with the members of the clique. Also, an actual physical fight can warrant calling the police to drag the perpetrators out of the building. The police are not responding to "subtle bullying," however. Girls can be extremely vicious, and they won't stop because they were simply "talked to."

10

The Powder-Puff Bowl: State-Sanctioned Barbarism

As a parent of a high school student, if you received a parental release form for your child to participate in a school-sponsored sport activity with the following cautionary statement, how would you react?

"I agree to accept any and all risks of injury, death, and/or property damage…"

Wait, don't react just yet, for the moment, keep reading.

As an example of the extremely vicious side to adolescent females, witness one of the most curious yet widely accepted "sport" activities in American high schools for more than fifty years—the annual powder-puff football game. It has no equal for viciousness among school- supported activities, and it draws many spectators, including young men and parents, anxious to see this violent behavior, because many guys still, unfortunately, like to watch females in physical conflict. Apparently, it has some deeply prurient aspect to it, and it is these spectators who help to encourage this vicious and demeaning loosely defined "football game" that many people like to pass off as a mere right of passage.

"Football is a rough sport, what do you expect?" is the excuse that these enablers of violence and mayhem hide behind—as if anything actually resembling football in its rule structure is about to take place.

In the next three pages, we ask the reader to examine the permission slips and other cautionary directions laid out by the various schools for the participants in this annual event. We will attempt to describe what we are reading as we peruse these documents.

First of all, we can safely say that all the participants in these games nationwide were probably athletes and played some other sport in their lives. But if they did not, then the point about to be mentioned has even more significance. If we assume that these young ladies played a sport, have they—or the boys, for that matter—ever had their parents agree to sign a permission slip to play that included the following:

Figure 1.

> If you are caught sending derogatory emails and/ or massages (incl. Facebook posts) to a member of another Anchor Club, you will not be eligible to play in the game…

Or, in p. 2:

> And then the release form of which we spoke at the outset, e.g., "I agree to accept any and all such risks of injury, *death*, and/or property damage…"

And finally:

> I waive, release, absolve, indemnify, and agree to hold harmless DHS, its members, officers, directors, employees, volunteers, agents, or other representative of DHS against any and all causes of action, claims, demands, losses, expenses, ability. In addition, if my conduct, if deemed inconsistent with the rules of good sportsmanship and fair play, etc., etc."

Sportsmanship and *fair play*? Really? After signing my child's life away to an activity that mentions the possibility of *death*? Did any of you or anyone you know of ever play a sport where any such verbiage was used in the sign-up process? Could it be that it was more or less understood that one's respect for football-wrestling-baseball-soccer-field hockey and the expected behavior of the participants assured everyone that no such words were needed to be a participant?

Powder Puff Behavior Contract

Due to the poor behavior of many girls in years past (some from each team), we have instituted a new rule in relation to Powder Puff. The rule (which all Anchor sponsors have agreed to enforce) is as follows:

If you are caught sending derogatory emails and/or messages (including Facebook posts) to a member of another Anchor club, you will not be eligible to play in the game. It should go without saying that you are representing not only yourself, but your school and the Anchor Club. While we want the girls to have a competitive spirit, this can be accomplished without being disrespectful to others.

Anchor Member:

I understand that if I am caught sending derogatory emails and/or messages (including Facebook posts) regarding Powder Puff Football, I will lose my eligibility to play in the game.

_____   _____
Anchor Signature   Date

Parent/Guardian:

I understand that if _____ is caught sending derogatory emails and/or messages (including Facebook posts) regarding Powder Puff Football, she will lose her eligibility to play in the game.

_____   _____
Parent/Guardian Signature   Date

Figure 1, p. 2 Note in p. 2 of Figure 1 the clause related to death. This is a school-sponsored activity.

POWDERPUFF PERMISSION SLIP/WAIVER FORM

WAIVER, RELEASE, COVENANT NOT TO SUE & INDEMNITY AGREEMENT

I understand and accept that there are risks involved in participating in any recreational activity. I am aware of those risks, and I am voluntarily participating in this activity with knowledge of the risks involved. I agree to accept any and all such risks of injury, death and/or property damage. I agree to the terms of this waiver, release, covenant not to sue and indemnity agreement as set forth herein. In case of injury or illness, I give my consent to emergency transportation and the administration of first aid, medical and/or dental treatment. I accept responsibility for the payment of any emergency transportation, treatment expenses and any related or subsequent medical and/or dental bills. I acknowledge that Draughn High School Anchor Club has not purchased and does not provide any medical or accident insurance to cover such expenses. Any such insurance is my responsibility. I waive, release, absolve indemnify and agree to hold harmless DHS, its members, officers, directors, employees, volunteers, agents or any other representative of DHS against any and all causes of action, claims, demands, losses, expenses, ability. In addition, I understand that my conduct, if deemed inconsistent with the rules of good sportsmanship and fair play, or the DHS Rules and Regulations may result in my expulsion from this and other programs.

I have fully read this document and understand it's meaning and legal impact. I voluntarily, of my own free will and without distress or coercion sign this waiver, release, covenant not to sue and indemnity agreement.

Student Name (Please Print) _____

Parent Name (Please Print)_____

Parent's Signature:_____

Date:_____

Sport: <u>Powder Puff Football</u>

Team Name: <u>DHS Anchor Club</u>

Figure 2.

The Manheim Township form reminds participants of the district's unlawful harassment policy. There also is a consent form for a urinalysis! We wonder if these words are on the forms for any other type of student activity—sports or otherwise—that the district sponsors. Keep in mind that these are some of the school's top students.

We read on: The high school "condemns all unwelcome and uninvited physical, verbal or non-verbal acts that are personally offensive and fail to respect the rights of others…" Does it bother anyone the lengths a school district will go to sponsor something as potentially dangerous as this? In other words, the lawyers tell them to include this verbiage, and it never begs the obvious question: "Why are we doing this in the first place?"

Manheim Township School District
Lancaster, Pennsylvania 17601

CONSENT TO MANDATORY RANDOM TESTING OF URINE SAMPLES
AND AUTHORIZATION FOR RELEASE OF INFORMATION

I hereby acknowledge that I have received information on the Manheim Township School District Drug Screening Policy. I further acknowledge that I have reviewed the information and that I fully understand the provisions of the drug testing program and agree to comply with the terms and conditions set forth in the Policy.

I hereby consent and authorize the School District to collect a urine sample from my student and to have such sample tested for the presence of certain drugs and substances in accordance with the provisions of the Policy. I further authorize the School District to release confidential information related to the drug screening to the approved contractor, school principal, District Superintendent or designee, athletic director, the head coach, director or club sponsor/advisor of any interscholastic sport or club in which my student participates and/or members of the Student Assistance Program, all information and records, including without limitation the results of the drug screening or testing of my student's urine in accordance with the Policy. To the extent set forth in this Consent, I waive any privilege with regard to such information.

I hereby acknowledge that this Consent shall remain valid unless and until I notify the School District in writing of my desire to remove my student from the School District's drug testing policy.

I hereby release and discharge, for myself and my student, the School District and its directors, officers, employees and agents from and of all claims, rights, expenses, debts, demands, costs, contracts, liability, obligations, actions, and causes of action of every nature, known or unknown, whether in law or equity, which I or my student had, now has, or may have which is in any way connected with, or arises out of the drug screening process or the Policy.

_____   _____   _____
Printed Student Name   Student Signature   Date

_____   _____   _____
Printed Parent/Guardian Name   Parent/Guardian Signature   Date

_____   _____
School Building   Extracurricular/Co-curricular Activity

That's right, folks, mandatory urine testing for the powder-puff bowl!

Figure 3. Woodcreek HS, paragraph 3 reads, "I understand that if my student commits an offense that would normally cause suspension from school while participating in the activity my child will be immediately removed from the activity, in addition to facing suspension from school…"

When was the last time a document like this was a part of the wrestling or football team processes or procedures?

Is this the theater of the absurd? Are schools really that worried about offending people that they lack the guts to end this activity once and for all? Circa 1908, President Theodore Roosevelt banned college football because there were too many head injuries. You can look it up. The hero of San Juan Hill and big game hunting, the man who took on the big corporations, something no president in his right mind would do today. He canceled college football because it was too rough. Now that took courage. My, how times have changed!

Permission Slip and Medical Authorization
Woodcreek High School Powder Puff Football

Student's Name:_____
Activity: Powder Puff Football   April 10 – April 20, 2012

I understand that this is a school-approved function and that my child must obey all rules of the school and remain under the supervision of those in charge.

I hereby release the school authorities from responsibility for accident or injuries which may occur due to the negligence or disobedience of my child.

I understand that if my student commits an offense which would normally cause suspension from the school while participating in this activity my child will be immediately removed from the activity, in addition to facing suspension from the school.

In the event of a medical emergency in which I cannot be contacted , school officials have my permission to seek medical assistance at my expense. Should there be an emergency, the following information is vital:

_____,   (_____)_____
Family Physician or Health Care Provider   Phone Number

My child has the following medical problems: (ie diabetes, asthma, heart problems, anaphylactic bee-sting allergy, etc...)

I, the undersigned, being the legal guardian of _____do hereby grant to any hospital, emergency center, doctor, nurse, and or paramedic authorization to grant treatment to my child when accompanied by or escorted to the treating facility by a teacher, coach, teacher's aide, principal, or any member of the Powder Puff Committee.

Further, should the attending physician determine after examination that life-saving surgery or other life-saving procedures may be necessary, permission is hereby extended to the above parties to grant same.

Additionally, I agree to hold harmless such personnel and Woodcreek High School by my action of granting said permission.

I declare under penalty of perjury that the above is true and correct.

_____   _____
      Date   Signature of Parent or Guardian

                          _____
                                          Address

                          _____
                          City   Zip   Phone

Figure 4. As the final example, here are some of the do's and don'ts from Bullitt Central HS:

Item #7 – "If you engage in any physical violence (fighting, scratching (!?), EYE-GOUGING Seriously? Where are you now, Chief Jay Strong Bow, the Iron Sheik, et al.?], BITING EARS What? Mike Tyson is smiling somewhere, you will be ejected from the game and suspended from school."

Thank goodness, at least people will be ejected if they bite somebody's ears! I'll sleep better knowing *that* provision is included! This is called mayhem in the law, ladies and gentlemen. You are going to jail for biting someone's ears. A number of sports would punish the offender with a lifetime ban from playing. That it even appears on a form designed to inform "nice" high school girls about the rules of the game is a disgrace. And yet the powder-puff game continues everywhere in the United States. No sports activity anywhere comes with these cautionary comments to which a parent must agree to sign his or her name. Gladiatorial contests in Ancient Rome came with greater anticipatory participant decorum. At least the gladiatorial contestants bowed to the emperor and were expected to act with decorum, even though death was a frequent expectation.

Powder Puff Practice and Game Schedule

1. Sanctioned school practices will be held on Monday, Tuesday and Wednesday, September 9th, 10th, and 11th at 6:00 PM on the softball outfield for Freshman and Senior girls. The Sophomores and Juniors will practice on the baseball outfield. DO NOT COME TO THE FOOTBALL FIELD AND DISTURB FOOTBALL PRACTICE.

2. The first game will be between the Freshmen and Juniors and will be played after the Homecoming Parade at 7:00 PM. The Sophomores and Seniors will play directly after the 1st game is finished at approximately 8:00 PM. The winners will meet in the championship game to be held on Friday during 6th period (1:05-2:05 PM).

3. You must wear a mouthpiece.

4. You cannot wear cleats.

5. Belts must be clearly visible at all times.

6. Sweats, T-shirts, etc. **are not** provided by Coach Gossett. There can be no profanity on the outfits. **Seniors will wear gray, Juniors will wear maroon, Sophomores will wear white, and Freshmen will wear black.** T-shirts can have any number you choose on the back.

    ***Proud Mamma Decals is offering a special $10 deal for Powder Puff team shirts at KYTshirts.com, or you can call owner Mike Dennis at 428-7474 for more information. These shirts can be personalized with your name and number.**

7. If you engage in any physical violence (fighting, scratching, eye gouging, biting ears, etc.) you will be ejected from the game and suspended from school. This is a school related activity, and we expect you to act as such.

8. Blocking is allowed, but you cannot reach out and grab an opponent at any time. Arms must be folded in front of you at all times if blocking.

9. The game will be divided into two twenty-minute halves. The clock will run continuously unless a time out is called or the officials stop the clock. There will be no exceptions to this rule.

10. You cannot wear jewelry of any kind.

11. You will be provided with a jersey. **You must give it back directly after the game.** You cannot pick a number, because I do not know which jersey numbers we have available for all levels.

12. If someone is coming to watch you play, admission will be $2.00 at the gate.

13. Each class must have a faculty sponsor to come watch each practice. The sponsor does not have to coach, but they must be present for Monday, Tuesday, and Wednesday's practice and Thursday and Friday for the game. Beg your teachers to help out.

Here are some of the newspaper reports on various powder-puff games around the nation. Still think girls are not at least as vicious as the boys? Read on…

Writing satirically, Kathleen Parker, a syndicated columnist for the *Orlando Sentinel*, said this about the school-sponsored powder-puff fracas in a suburban Chicago high school in 2003:

> Girls will be girls—give them a couple of kegs, some pig intestines, and a bucket of human feces and, well, stuff happens! So goes the attitude out there passing for commentary following the brutal powder-puff melee in which senior girls attacked juniors during a "traditional hazing rite." Seen any football games with feces and pig entrails being smooshed in the faces of the participants? Do any school people have enough courage to end this degrading and life-threatening activity?
>
> Pig entrails? It's time for our school leaders and their enabling and entitled parents to get a grip.

The *Minneapolis Star Tribune* had this to say about a nearby annual powder-puff classis:

> Saying they are fed up with vandalism, foul language, and rough play, NP School officials may wash their hands of a homecoming tradition- The powder-puff football game. The Fall event has gotten too violent and rowdy said Principal Tom D. Its supposed to be Touch Football and people are tackling one another without equipment. Also, the concept of "Class Spirit" has gone too far with people DAMAGING HOMES AND CARS in the days before the game.

USA Today offered this review of a recent "game":

Officials at Glenbrook North HS in Northbrook Ill. Were examining videotapes by students following the powder-puff football game between Junior and Senior girls. They were expecting to see an actual game, but instead they saw Junior girls beaten, splattered with paint and their faces smeared with feces. "I guess there was some football involved," said the Superintendent, "but then it all pushing, punching, hitting, putting buckets on people's heads, and showering people with debris and human excrement."

Just a right of passage, folks? Read on…

The *New York Times* reported on a powder-puff bowl game in Westport, Connecticut, going all the way back to December of 1985 with the following:

In some cases, girls were put on a "hit list" and opposing seniors went after them physically. Students came to be spectators so they could witness the violence and encourage the violence. Several participants suffered physical injuries and broken bones. In another school district, the Student Council President and some of his minions were arrested for trashing the home of several of the players while they were at the game! They received a $250 fine. I guess they were just kids having fun and stuff! What could ever motivate young people to completely "lose their minds" like this in the hoopla surrounding a student activity?

But wait, the principal at a suburban Boston high school has canceled the annual game saying it is sexist, divisive, and dangerous. A stroke of sanity perhaps in this cowardly zeitgeist?

There were five reasons why the tradition was ended, and some principals, perhaps to cover themselves and look noble, are quick to say that such a game "perpetuates negative stereotypes about femininity and female athletes owing in large part to the term *powder-puff*, which describes something that my mom used to have on her dresser to powder her nose, in a round, hard candy–sized tin filled with exotic-smelling powder, usually with a French name. Believe me, the principal just wants to get rid of this abomination in any way he can, but resorting to political correctness is searching pretty deep for cover.

The principal went on to say that the term *powder-puff* inadvertently serves to mock the hard-fought struggles of female athletes to be taken seriously and, we think, perpetuates blah-blah-blah. (The "hard-fought struggles" part is a nice turn of phrase—you can almost hear the violins playing.) Other throw-in reasons—the real ones—were *injuries* (there, he said the real one!) and maintenance of an "intimidation-free school environment." Well, let's just give the man credit for ending this abomination. I wonder if it was the first year or the last year of the superintendent's contract—but that's a discussion for another day!

Folks, if you are serious about ending bullying and creating an intimidation-free environment, then fill the room at the school board meeting, and keep filling it, plan on getting tossed out, and keep bugging them till they end it once and for all. A little civil disobedience brings out the media and forces the superintendent to address a matter. If you don't think extreme measures are required to fix this, then stop pretending you care about bullying.

11

Wait! What about Hazing?

Item: A child in kindergarten is expelled from school for creating something shaped like a gun from a piece of bread. Another child in the primary grades is expelled for having a small pair of scissors. The powder-puff game is still on the calendar, though; and in the world's greatest exhibition of selective supervision, the ninth graders on a private school football team near Chicago are beaten with belts by varsity players, *and* their coaches. And this time they are caught, though everyone knew that this had happened before.

In Colorado, three upperclassmen on a wrestling team duct-tape a ninth grader and sodomize him with a pencil. The ninth grader was the son of the high school principal. Two of the attackers were sons of Robert Harris, the wrestling coach, who was also the school board president. The principal correctly reported the incident to the police. Students and townspeople protested *against* the victim and his father the principal, forcing the principal to resign. In school, "Go to Hell" stickers were on the victim's locker, and students wore T-shirts that communicated their support for the perpetrators. The attackers would later plead guilty to misdemeanor charges only. The ex-principal would only say that no one in the area who was a lawyer would help.

Apparently, we have come a long way from having the ninth graders sing the alma mater and have to carry the water containers out to practice. Hazing has been around since the really old days, and everyone has a story—everyone— and that story is that of a victim or a perpetrator. Why is hazing okay? Well, for one thing, no one sees or hears it when a team is winning. Sometimes, when the team starts losing, people take notice. The main point is that hazing is almost always sport or fraternity related, and it's been historically considered more of a rite of passage than just plain bullying, but not by much. Also, if there was ever a case of selective observation going on, it's in high school sports programs, where the coach and his staff simply play dumb. As was mentioned, everyone has a story. Here are some that have appeared in the newspapers in the last ten years or so. It's amazing how everyone is either "shocked and appalled" when a story comes out, or mad at the exposer of the truth. Read on.

Apparently, being sodomized is relatively common in the world of hazing. Outside Los Angeles, several boys were *raped* (it is rape when penetration against someone's will or to someone underage occurs—even a slight amount) with a broken flagpole. In Fontana, California, the act was done with a reinforcing bar. In Greenfield, Iowa, the *Bloomberg*

News reported that it was done with a jump rope handle; and in Hardin, Missouri, with a water bottle.

While little research has been done on boy-on-boy sexual hazing (because few will talk about it), 10% of high school males report hazing that was sexual and criminal, from oral sex to rape with foreign objects to horrible things like "teabagging," meaning people rubbing their scrotums across the victim's face. Ask your athlete son if he ever heard the word *teabagging* and what it means. Play dumb, and listen closely. This came from a study in 2009 in the *Journal of Youth and Adolescence*.

William Pollack is an associate professor of psychology at Harvard. He asserts that high school boys have a need to display their manliness, and they do it by humiliating younger boys because that is what they think demonstrates manliness.

The US Department of Education reported to educators that over 4,000 sexual assaults occur each year in public school including 800 rapes or attempted rapes. Stating that nowhere else in society is this kind of behavior tolerated, Antonio Romanucci, an attorney, demands to know why, in high school sports, it is tolerated, only being put to an end when it is finally discovered.

Robert Kennedy, writing on About.com, asserts that hazing exists quite simply because parents, teachers, coaches, and students allow it to exist. As harsh as it may sound, no one wants to do or say something that might affect his son or daughter and their ability to play on a team—it might affect their playing time, is one concern. Traditions force people to look the other way. Coaches leave the room and allow the upperclassmen to "do their thing." When parents demand zero tolerance regarding hazing, not to mention the powder-puff football game, it will finally go away. Don't hold your breath waiting for that to happen, though. Yet we still want to expel the kindergarten kid with the pop tart shaped like a gun.

Every movie that has a new coach coming to town, like *Hoosiers*, for example, show the new coach meeting before the tribunal of good old boys at Luke's Barber Shop or Mom's Restaurant and get read the riot act about "how we do things around here."

Here's the thing: hazing is illegal in almost every state, but not in all of them. Alaska, Montana, South Dakota, Hawaii, New Mexico, and Wyoming may have zero tolerance rules in place for nail files, but not for hazing. No one should assume that all the organizations in the school are free from hazing. Remember, if practical jokes, insults, exclusions, and rumors constitute bullying in the school's bullying policy, please explain why hazing in sports and the powder-puff bowl with pig entrails and feces rubbed in one's face are ignored. Here is how you know it is ignored: because it is not brought to an end till it is exposed in the media and perpetrators are threatened with lawsuits.

The *Huffington Post* makes a cogent argument when it refers to the Don't Ask Don't Tell policy that underlies all high school sports programs. Students who are bystanders must from an early age be praised and celebrated for coming forth with the truth. When people ignore the indignities being visited on students, those indignities will continue without end—until a tragedy occurs. Then the problem is finally addressed and a school moves past decontextualized lip service.

12

The Biggest Myths about Bullying

For most people, their thoughts about school are profoundly affected by their own school experiences, thus there are grandparents around who will still say things like, "If we got in trouble at school, we would get it again from Mom and Dad when we got home because the teacher and the school were always right."

Or perhaps, if you fight with the bully, he won't bother you anymore. Even the struggles involving bullies in our lives are a part of growing up, and it helps to "toughen us up." Additionally, no one in the day ever thought that girls would be bullies. It was generally understood that you did not squeal about the bully to anyone, because things like practical jokes, punches to the shoulder, getting stuffed in a locker, having books knocked out of your hands, being given a wedgie, being called a "fag" or a "homo," having a "Kick me" sign put on your back, girls having lewd and immoral stories told about them, etc., were all simply a part of growing up, so "get over it, you baby!"

The myths that exist, then, are a combination of our past experiences of how things were and a complete lack of understanding of what is actually going on in school these days. Your grandparents and the ladies in the cafeteria think that if school people just kicked a little more butt, these things would not happen anyway. Many of those people want educators carrying guns in the school building too.

Let's take a look, then, at some of the most predominant myths about bullying in the lives of young people.

Adults don't behave this way!

Are you paying attention to the news with anyone who is different? Gays, people of color, Islamic people, poor people being marginalized or treated as though they "deserve" their plight? Television shows with British people cursing at and calling everyone obscene names, sitcoms that portray dads as idiots (especially black dads), kids being considered cute and funny for the various practical jokes they play on adults, the greatest amount of fiendish laughter on funny home video shows being when a middle-aged woman slips and falls, Dad takes one in the groin at the piñata party, or someone is "catfished" or scared out of their minds by someone. Admit it, folks, this is why most of us men can't get enough of the Three Stooges—they are constantly beating on each other or insulting one another. The cartoons are the same way with Elmer Fudd, Wile E. Coyote, and Sylvester the Cat always coming up on the short side of things. Most of you will not remember that funny television shows disrespectful to adults go back to about 1955 with *The Andy Devine Show*. Andy Devine would have a variety of puppet characters in the show, and there was always a lady like Julia Child explaining how to bake a cake or a nutty professor showing his secret formula, and they would always be interrupted and confused by the antics of Froggy Gremlin or some other character, to the roaring laughter of children in the audience. Who of us adults does not love those Three Stooges classics or other such shows with the inevitable pie fight that would start and the especially uppity old ladies would get it in the face with a pie. We all grew up on that stuff and loved every minute of it. Groucho Marx made a career out of insulting the pompous Margaret Dumont, to the delight of your grandparents.

In England, for example, there is a workplace law against bullying. Not in the United States, though, where the boss is supposed to be an ass kicker a la John Wayne. Sorry, folks, the kids learn this stuff from you, and all of us adults were just as bad as the kids are now. Remember Mischief Night. It started out with soaping windows. Then I moved to Willow Grove, Pennsylvania, and there were three nights: Chalk Night, Soap Night, and the regular Mischief Night. However, communities across the country have created their own bullying traditions. When I got to my first principal job in Millville, Pennsylvania, there was no actual Mischief Night. Instead, all the high school kids, or those who thought they were too old to do any trick or treating, ran through the town leaving the trick-or-treaters alone but attacking one another with toothpaste, eggs, shaving cream, toilet paper, and all sorts of smelly things. When I asked about this curious activity, the response was much like that of Tevye in *Fiddler on the Roof*: "We don't know how it got started, but it's a tradition."

Also, I was told, "They are just kids having fun," and "nobody is actually hurting anyone." Besides, since everyone is involved, it's a "fair fight." I guess that is a bit different from a clear-cut victim and a clear-cut perpetrator, with no bystanders. However, when I was in town with my trick-or-treater boys, I saw certain less popular individuals being the most frequently attacked target. But: "Okay," I replied to the enabling adults, and moved on incredulously.

To be real, the bullying must actually be physical.

This is the notion held by many of us senior citizens, and it is enforced every Christmas when we see twenty-four hours of *The Christmas Story* with Ralphie and friends running away from archetypal bullies Scut Farkus and Grover Dill who inflict physical harm on them. Those are the kind of bullies I remember. Wayne Fochler and Carl Ewing were my Scut Farcas growing up. However, by now, most of us agree that in the electronic age, great damage can be done to another without raising a fist.

According to the Human Rights Education Center, bullying is when one child regularly harasses another child.

We disagree, of course, and would immediately remove *regularly* from their definition. Remember, in the law, you don't have to rob somebody multiple times before you are called a robber and convicted of robbery. That said, they assert that the bullying could be verbal bullying, like the British chefs who curse at and insult everyone on TV. Just an aside: did you or your family ever say, "Hey, let's go out for some British food"? Funny how they became the food experts…but we digress once again. It can include name-calling, teasing, and the use of threatening language. It can also be electronic—via texting, Twitter, the Internet, etc. Children know how to put a survey online about "Who is the biggest slut in the school?" from home, and parents will come storming into school wanting to sue the district as if we at the school can control what happens at their house!

However, when a child is constantly not chosen into a game or excluded at other social events, does that amount to bullying? Under the new definition, we would strongly argue, *yes*! In the old days, when I was a sixth-grader, Eileen Wilson would get thirty-one Valentine's cards. I usually got about twelve or fifteen. We would laugh at Frankie Schultz, who usually got one or two. What do you think about Valentine cards in school? Do we do away with them, let kids give them to whom they wish to like in the old days, or be made to give a card to everyone? Sounds unimportant, yet a child could truly be scarred for life by the dreaded

Valentine's Day party. You probably did not think of that institutional aspect of potential bullying.

Here are the statistics that the Human Rights Education Center provided regarding the ways students have been bullied.

-21% said they have been called names, insulted, or made fun of

-18% reported being the subject of rumors

-11% said they were pushed, shoved, tripped, or SPIT ON!

-6% said they were threatened by harm

- 4% said they were made to do things against their will

-4% said their property was destroyed on purpose- (like that piece of pizza placed in a brand new social studies book)

There is a high correlation between physical size and bullying.

This implies that shorter, skinnier "weaklings" are the ones that are the targets, and the big guys tend to be the bullies. However, bullying is more often a psychological matter rather than a physical one. Experts assert that bullying is about power, and the bullying is related to another problem in the life of the bully. Thus, the bully could very well be a smaller person. Size is not the most distinguishing factor. Witness the 300-plus-pound offensive lineman on the Miami Dolphins who has sued another player and the team for bullying and its painful emotional effect on his ability to play the game. You can be big and be bullied. When I was teaching in the high school, there was always at least a dozen boys walking the halls who were six foot five or taller and never touched a basketball. When I asked them the inevitable question "Why aren't you a basketball player?" the answer was always the same: "In the middle school, I was way taller than everyone and uncoordinated. The kids and/or the teacher/coach teased me constantly about being a geek or a nerd. Now I am a rocker/goth/hipster, and I hate sports!"

Stand and fight the bully…When he realizes that the target is too much work to terrorize, he'll find someone else to bully.

My dad and your dad told us to "be a man" and "stand your ground" and "fight back" because "I don't want people to think my son is a wuss." Ever hear that kind of advice or, worse yet, give out that kind if advice? In the old days, this advice had perhaps slightly more merit, but today, with kids bringing weapons to school and seeking never-ending revenge, fighting back is not the best advice. One expert compares it to an arms race, with the weapons and the posses getting bigger and bigger. What happens when a child uses self-defense in school? Is the punishment the same for both fighters regardless of the reason owing to the politicians' masterpiece, the zero tolerance policy? "An eye for and eye makes the whole world blind," asserted Ghandi. There are many more effective ways to deal with bullies. In the final chapter, we discuss some useful individual and collective strategies in an effort to make bullying go away.

If you ignore the bullying, eventually, it will go away.

Bullying is a reflection of the imbalance of power between the bully and the victim. Bullies learn fast. If there is nothing done to stop the bully, the peaceful actions of the victim are simply viewed as weakness. The bully realizes that he can terrorize this person without consequences. Consequences or the possibility of consequences will usually deter a bully. Machiavelli spoke about the importance of "a few signal examples" to impact public opinion. A student or two taken out of the building in handcuffs with a lot of people around can work wonders. That is why the local police are mad at you if they stop you for speeding and you pull off into a parking lot so their "show" is less effective.

You can feel sure that trained teachers will know what is going on and intervene on behalf of the victim.

Since most adults sound like good supervisors with loud voices and big muscles, the average person can think that things in this supervised area are under control. However, for reasons spoken of in this book, only 14% of the time are teachers sharp enough to grasp what is really happening and therefore able to prevent the bullying in the first place.

One sure way to end the bullying is to call the bully's parents.

Often, the involvement of parents with one another in the bullying process can get especially heated and ugly. Rather than getting drawn into the parent-to-parent battle, experts suggest starting at the school and have the school personnel sit in at the meeting. It's not an even affair, however. Too often, the school people will try to act like a mediator. Mediation assumes that two sides are equally into the fray, which they are not. One person is always the victim, and these kinds of meetings can make it look that everyone is in the same position. Make it clear to the school official that it is your child who is the victim, and that before you go to a lawyer, you are kindly giving the school official the opportunity to deal with the problem. However, if the false equivalence approach is used by the school, the parent will have to make it clear that the next person they visit will be a lawyer.

It is mostly just boys who bully.

A survey from 2007 revealed that 34% of girls reported being bullied and 31% of boys said they were bullied. People will say, "Yes, but the girls don't often resort to physical bullying." Wrong! Ask any principal who has ninth graders in his building. Even the boys are scared of the ninth-grade girls, and they will resort to physical attacks, sometimes more quickly than boys. However, it is accurate that girls are more skilled at exclusion, rumors, name-calling, and other indirect forms of bullying. Surveys entitled "Who is the biggest slut in the school" are often the work of girls, as it seems that boys just don't care enough to spend that kind of time hurting others. Ask any adult female about mean girl bullying, and they will tell you how nasty it really can be. If parents find that their daughter is acting sad, depressed, feigning illness, or using other reasons to avoid school, seek the help of the school counselor or someone else who can talk with the girl if she seems unwilling to talk with her parents. Suicides that were in some way caused by bullying appear to be more frequent with girls. Indirect bullying can be devastating.

Schools are often unfairly the fall guy for bullying problems that happen mostly out of school.

This is very inaccurate for reasons spoken of in this book. What might appear to a hall monitor as a peaceful situation may not be at all, because the supervisor is just a big, scary person with a loud voice and it does not seem as though bullying is happening. Too often, this is exactly the place bullies do their best work, because they know when the guard does not "get it."

Parents of a bullied child need to do as mentioned previously and let the school know that they are being kind enough to respectfully give the school a chance to correct this problem. Then they will be visiting a lawyer. Parents are advised to mark down the time and date they meet with school officials, and they should send a letter, with copies to the superintendent, stating the resolution they expect to achieve with this meeting.

Alert parents usually know when their children are the victims of bullying.

False! Most children, especially after elementary school, don't want to tell their parents anything that is going on in school, least of all that they might be being bullied. I have had parents in my office saying, "My child would never lie to me!" Then I would show them the video from the school bus showing that their child clearly did lie to them. Another famous lie that a child will tell is that their expensive new leather jacket that they lost at the mall on Sunday was stolen from their locker in the locker room.

Getting back to the point: children lie. They lie frequently, and when they know they can manipulate Mom or Dad, they will tell whatever story they need to get Mom or Dad to help fight the battle. Many children carry on the charade for a very long time, and parents are shocked to find out how long the problem has been going on. As a principal, each year there were parents who were shocked to find that their child might not graduate because of extremely low grades. I would ask it these parents ever spoke to their child about how they were doing in school since they see the child every night. They still thought the problem was the school's.

If an angry parent comes in to express a concern about a long-standing bullying problem, they will not be mad at their child for hiding it or lying about it. Misplaced aggression will result in those parents wanting to know why the school did not get to the bottom of this sooner. The school must, for that reason, create incentives for staff to be on top of their respective games when they are supervising or when they are simply engaging students in conversation—something they should always be encouraged to do so they can find out this valuable information and solve the matter early rather than later. Schools are, sadly, seldom proactive, but great at having wonderful speakers and other programmatic changes, but often after a problem or in response to a felt need.

The social media sites are like toothpaste out of the tube—you can't get it back in. Kids can become like Frankenstein in the old movie, where all the townspeople are about to burn the child at the stake. They are the modern-day electronic lynch mobs. When things go viral, suicides can, and do, happen. A tough guy school employee does not equal a proactive one. Our efforts must be targeted at heightening everyone's awareness about how and where these things happen and who is the perpetrator.

Bullies come from the top of the social pecking order and are usually the cool kids.

Social gain is clearly a goal of almost 95% of bullying. Thus, if the bully were at the top of some social order, why would they need to bully? They are already cool. Experts Mayer and Williams assert that bullying is almost always motivated by a desire for social power. A bully has the ability to manipulate the social order and may be jealous of his victim's social standing.

Another common issue facing bullies is that they have often been the victim of abuse themselves, and their actions of bullying others may be a cry for help. Anyone wielding power in an inappropriate way has probably had the same thing happen to them. It often indicates a lack of control in his or her life. Issues in the home such as divorce, addiction, abuse, and violence leave children in a helpless state. The saying often stated is that "hurt people hurt people." Are you a school administrator? Try to remember that the juvenile justice system is built on a rehabilitative model, not a punitive one. That means we are trying to help people who have problems to make their problems go away. Putting a bully in a room of children with autism and telling the child that he will be helping these students as part of his community service can produce amazing results. More about this in the next chapter.

13

Where Do We Go from Here?
Any Solutions?

Are there solutions to this problem of bullying? We return to the first sentence about definitions being tricky things with inconvenient truths. We spoke about changing definitions to improve perceptions and lower costs. Recently, the "problem" of special education budgets was aided by politicians. How? As stated, they simply changed the definition of autism spectrum disorder and the kind of "special needs" a student must have in order to receive special services. How convenient! Thus, we can improve things like test scores, dropout rates, absenteeism, reports of bullying, etc., by just changing the definition.

In Vietnam, a strategy recommended was to simply "declare victory and go home." The politicians and the media have done this before by creating perceptions. The announcement to you on TV that with "2% of the precincts reporting we are about to declare a winner" during some previous Presidential Election probably has kept a large number of people overtime from even running down to the polls to vote in the last half hour before they closed. Witness one part of the political spectrum today, and the first thing on their list to balance the budget is to eliminate school breakfast programs and revise the family income levels needed to qualify for free and reduced lunch. Watch for more of these definition revisions. The road ahead will be bumpy for victims of anything, let alone bullying.

According to Elsea and Smith, the definition of bullying has been different for the children being bullied than for the adults who write the definitions since records have been kept on the issue. Typically, the difference of opinion involves how many times a victim must be bullied before the system recognizes this as bullying. From a public relations standpoint, it reflects well with a school district and for the realtors in the area if the negative metrics are low and the positive ones are high, unless a district has justified its lowered test scores by saying, for example, that the number of students on free and reduced lunch in their district is high. That is usually an indicator of less education on the part of parents, and thus, a child who will score lower on tests because he is not supported well by his parents—from a scholarly standpoint at least.

Institutions are concerned about their image. Witness the recent Penn State tragic fiasco or the issue with priests in the Catholic church. For our purposes, it should be made clear that to students, and undoubtedly to their parents, one incident of bullying is bullying. How insensitive and institutionally protective it is to make an act of bullying not count as bullying until there is a "pattern." Who makes the determination about what constitutes a pattern? At the current rate of insensitivity by our elected officials, a year might have to pass before a pattern emerges. Ask a child who has been the victim of physical or verbal abuse if he thinks this is bullying.

Another aspect of bullying definitions is that there must be a mens rea, or intent, on the part of the perpetrator for the act to amount to bullying. SooHoo posits that an overemphasis on intentionality as a prerequisite for bullying prevents reports of overaggressive acts from being reported or investigated if they are understood not to be intentional.

So first, a definition must be recognized that makes bullying count as bullying the *first* time it happens. Seriously, does burglary need repeated occurrences to be burglary? What about rape, child molestation, larceny? In the law, it is larceny the second your hand moves an object that does not belong to you if you had the intent to take it. But we are willing to allow children to be abused for a while until it becomes official?

After the definition is accurately written, the staff needs specialized training beyond their size and loud voice and nasty face that they can make to strike fear in the hearts of the miscreants. Olweus asserts that it is essential in any bullying program that the adults at the school must become aware of the extent of the bully/victim problems in their own school. This amounts to discernment and also honesty. Many school districts in more affluent communities are very image conscious and play down the issue of bullying and the number of times the police are called for the number of suicide attempts that occur in their district.

An article from bullyonline, written and produced in England where, for example, workplace bullying laws have been in place for some years, makes the following bold assertion:

> Where a school claims that "There is no bullying here" that is where you are most likely to find bullying. Good schools are PROACTIVE in their approach and deal with incidents of bullying firmly and fairly. Bad schools deny it, ignore it, justify it, rationalize it, handle it inappropriately, sweep it under the carpet, blame the victim, blame the parents, … and make lots of impressive noises for their negligence and breach of the duty of care (Penn State syndrome). In most schools which claim "there's no bullying here," the primary objective is to protect the school against bad publicity and to divert attention away from the fact that the people in charge do not have control of discipline in the school. Even schools who appear in the news following a tragic event sometimes miss the point completely. When the terrible shooting tragedy occurred on the campus of Virginia Tech, the celebration and cheers about "Hokie Pride" and

how "you can't hurt us Hokies" during a memorial service for the dead showed great disrespect for those who lost someone in a bloody murder. The people were cheering as though it was a football game! The whole "Hokie Pride" pageantry following the disaster lacked the appropriate solemnity. The school was so quick to beat the drums for how it was not about to suffer from a disaster and how it was strong, so Dad should not worry but keep writing those checks—that they missed the focus completely. "Hokie Pride" was something to talk about months later, not coincident with real people who were now getting buried and their grieving families. Imagine yourself a parent with a child who was murdered in cold blood in a place where this is not supposed to happen. Would the fact that the school is staying strong and tough with a "Pep Rally" despite the tragedy be a comfort to you?

Before you make the usual assertion about how nasty kids are these days, take a look at the way the adults are acting. We don't know about you, but we do not recognize the country we grew up in anymore. Civility is in short supply these days—especially by those charged most seriously with exhibiting it. Fortunately, artists, writers, musicians, singers, and comedians have had the conscience for us all to act like the little boy in Aesop's fable "The Emperor's New Clothes" and say what is really going on when it needed to be said. People like Dr. Seuss (*The Sneetches and Other Stories*) Rodgers and Hammerstein/James Michener (*South*

Pacific), Henrik Ibsen (*An Enemy of the People*), the Chad Mitchell Trio, the song "Draft Dodger Rag," rap songs, and the list goes on. These people are heroes for telling it like it is. How is your conscience on this matter?

The world we live in is a difficult place. Life has never been more difficult in the United States than it is today for anyone unique or "different." Just look at all the American flags on the stores of Middle Eastern, Indian, and Pakistani merchants, for example. Children have learned all of the viciousness from the adults. That's right, folks. We adults all share the blame. We helped make the kids the way they are. Watch *America's Funniest Home Videos* as an example. In any film clip of older women getting hit, falling at a wedding, etc., or in any film clip of a small child having an unfortunate fall, getting knocked over by the dog, etc., the camera flashes to the audience, where people are cackling fiendishly at the plight of the less fortunate, and of course, witness the hilarity when Dad gets whacked by the mandatory-for-every-show bat in the groin when a blindfolded kid tries to hit that stupid piñata! Every commercial or family show with a black father portrays the man as an idiot while the mom is the brains of the family, and when a white dad is shown, all the children are laughing at him for his Archie Bunker–type mentality.

Arizona wants to make a wall, but no one wants a wall along the Canadian border. People tell Jewish, Italian, black, Polish, and blonde jokes…where are the English,

German, Danish, and Norwegian jokes? America's history of eugenics and social Darwinism (helping others less fortunate than you goes against the natural order of things) caused Hitler to stop and take notes in the 1930s and send his doctors here to learn more about the amazing American sterilization program. We are experts in this country at mistreating people and being mean. We are twenty-seventh in the industrialized world in infant mortality, and lower in income inequality. The Three Stooges are still the best thing on TV—at least for all you dads out there. Yet people are aghast at all of the bullying. Oscar Hammerstein (22) railed against the hatred years ago in the song, "You've Got to Be Taught" from *South Pacific*.

> You've got to be taught to hate and fear.
> You've got to be taught from year to year.
> It's got to be drummed in your dear little ear.
> You've got to be carefully taught.
> You've got to be taught to be afraid.
> Of people whose eyes are oddly made.
> And people whose skin is a different shade.
> You've got to be carefully taught.
> You've got to be taught before its too late.
> Before you are 6 or 7 or 8.
> To hate all the people your relatives hate.
> You've got to be carefully taught.
> You've got to be carefully taught.

The state of Georgia tried to get this show and this song banned as being "communistic," but the authors refused to budge. What great heroes!

Listen for a moment, all of you adults. Often, without even trying, we have managed to make sure our children have been "carefully taught to hate and fear." Does your child stay late at school to get help or help the teacher, or perhaps participate in something that is a bit undefined? Do they eat lunch in the library because they like to help the librarian? Has any teacher ever spoken to you about their lateness to class?

Constant and contextualized vigilance is all we have, folks. Children will usually not tell adults what is going on. Fancy cameras, metal detectors, dead bolt locks, school police, and legally perfect discipline codes are minor inconveniences to skilled bullies. People in jail are always closely supervised and always in a place where there are many people (the yard, cafeteria, workplace, etc.), yet brutal attacks occur regularly. The bullies, folks, are in plain sight; and their work goes undetected each day. And "maybe those damn hippies deserve it," as I remember an old John Wayne–type teacher say.

Can we fix it? Maybe. This book will speak to some suggestions that are different than the ones you have heard before. Yes, folks, schools are like the Wild West on steroids. We hope the book increases your awareness of the scope and depth of the problem and moves everyone past simple lip service about bullying because it is fashionable to talk about right now. Sinclair Lewis gave this definition of a politician: "One who is ample and vague on all subjects."

It is our hope that what you read here will be ample, but not vague as to what and where things are happening, as well as some suggestions for confronting the nightmare that kids face every day entering the school building.

In this vast play known as *Bullying*, there are three principal characters, namely, the Bully, the Victim, and the Bystander. In many of the strategies being discussed today, the person whose responsibility has grown significantly in the minds of experts and laymen alike is that of the Bystander. Keep these roles in mind, but put additional focus on the Bystander. It is this character who has been getting a free pass in the drama surrounding bullying.

The three main strategies being recommended today are clearly different from the old days in many ways, but some ideas have never changed. Here are some strategies to offer to those who are a victim that are appearing frequently in the literature and from so-called experts. The victim or the Bystander can try some of these strategies with some success:

Tell the Bully to stop what he/she is doing.

This might mean making a scene, as I did at the beach last summer when a manager in a coffee shop was yelling at a helpless, crying waitress in front of the customers. I told the man to cut it out and asked him if it wouldn't be a better idea to speak with the employee privately because the one coming out looking stupid in this outburst was him, not his employee, and that I was going to tell everyone I could find to avoid this store because the boss is such a cruel jerk.

He grumbled some expletive deleted under his breath and stopped yelling at the waitress. If you have ever owned Siamese cats, then by all means, take a lesson from them. Over fifteen years, whenever I had cause in my mind to raise my voice at the people sharing the house with me, I would have to quickly stop because the cats would confront me, sometimes right up in my face if I was on the couch, and start yelling back at me with their loud, menacing meow as if to say, "Knock it off, boss. You are acting like a jerk!" It always worked. I miss them a lot.

Tell an adult.

Kids tend to use this as a last resort based on their fear that a decontextualized adult paying only the slight interest in the complaint will lead to even further punishment by the Bully, because even if there is a punishment, it will be slight, and the Bully will only come back, this time angrier than before. Today, the responsibility for curing bullying has fallen upon the previously silent Bystander, who is now being encouraged to tell all the adults he or she can find. The person being bullied often does not share his plight with anyone—least of all his parents. Keep encouraging your child and everyone around him to bother the adults as much as possible with bullying reports. When the Bully sees no one is being entertained by his or her antics, when he or she notices that it is no longer "cool" here in this school, the bullying will stop. The act of telling an adult, then, has to be a team effort. Research has shown that where somebody else, a third party, steps in and tells the Bully to cut it out or the group think is to share this information with the authorities, the Bully tends to all but completely disappear since the Bully lacks an audience to play to.

Recently, on a Japanese television network, a program was being shown about a preschool in the mountains of Japan. In this particular preschool, children were encouraged to circle around a bully and continue to advise the bully calmly but with at least a slight scolding tone that what he or she was doing was not nice. It was amazing to see the contriteness of the bully when everyone around him was not entertained by his actions. Lacking an audience, the bully was embarrassed and stopped in his tracks.

Is this something we can begin to inculcate in our children at an early age, say, preschool, like the Japanese are using with apparent great success?

A publication entitled *Care Notes for Teens* offers this suggestion: "Talk to your parents. A bully," asserts the publication, "who is exposed is a little bit like the famous wizard in the classic movie *The Wizard of Oz*." Remember the phrase spoken by the Wizard when Dorothy and her entourage reach the castle's main chamber... Toto moves the curtain aside and the Wizard yells, "Ignore that man behind the curtain!"

Actually, the big tough Wizard was being exposed for the charlatan that he was. Bullies thrive on secrecy and reputation. They have a role to play; they need it to continue their act and their mystique. You must literally pull the curtain back on this charlatan and expose him or her. Your parents may not be able to protect you from every problem that life throws at you, but they are your most valuable friends, whether you realize it or not. The Bully needs you to keep the secret. As soon as you start talking to others about the problem, starting with your parents, that is precisely when the curtain falls away from the Bully. Your coach, minister, favorite teacher, guidance counselor also are there for you. Tell as many people as you can about what is going on.

Walk away.

Easy advice to give, but let's see you guidance counselors try it when you are being threatened. This one has some value but might not work depending on the situation. Suppose the Bully keeps pushing or hitting you? Turning the other cheek might be a noble thought, but without some friends around, this strategy might be doomed to failure. The power of having friends around, though, cannot be discounted.

Try not to react.

It is hard not to react. Sometimes, a victim might even need to cry. However, bullies feed on the scared reaction that a victim has. Keeping a straight face and walking into anyone's room, office, etc., will leave the Bully hanging. Even keeping a disinterested or bored look will confound the Bully even more.

Get into an organized group activity.

In his amazing book, *The Pursuit of Wow!*, the legendary Tom Peters advises his readers to "forget your enemies... Surround your enemies with your friends!" Indeed, when anyone is accepted to college, one of the first mailings to the incoming freshman after his or her letter of congratulations is the advice to join a club, a sport, an activity...something where you will have an immediate group of people around who look after one another. When you have a freshman English class with 300 students taught by a grad assistant for full price at the big university you had to attend, you'll understand loneliness.

Today in all the colleges, there are highly organized—complete with uniforms and coaches and buses—club sports teams. They are a great way to enjoy competition, a step down from the varsity, but with a great group of friends, and it's the only organized sport where there are no size categories. In other words, your baseball team at

Tankwater Tech can play Southern Cal in the club team finals for baseball held each year. How many of us old folks wish that club sports were like this back in the day, with real games and real officials and uniforms and practices and the usual camaraderie that come with sports participation.

However, every town and every school has music and drama groups. I have been in some amateur theater productions over the years. They were a great deal of fun, with amazing creative collaboration between diverse individuals where lifelong friends are made…Let me add that no one parties like show people. Try out for a play. Even if you wind up on the set crew or working as a prompter, you will be amazed at the parties these people have. Way beyond anything you've experienced in sports, I guarantee you. Guys, join a dance class. You heard me, a dance exercise class, to be precise. It will consist of 98 percent girls and you. Think about it. Enough said.

So, whether you are in high school, college, or any level, including the workplace, join a group that pursues some fun pastime! Don't suffer in silence, but be near people you can actually talk to.

For School Officials

Let's say it up front: Bullying is never going away. However, the situation can be significantly improved by supervision that comes with context—which is to say an awareness in advance of the time, the place, the actions that occur there, and the characters involved in the actions. The mental health professionals and the guidance counselors should be permitted to do what they do best—meeting with children in groups, pairs, and individually to discuss the ways in which people treat one another. Long-term strategies must be combined with those of a shorter term. Having "eyes" and a "nose" for things that might happen might be a skill taught best by the local or state police rather than a mental health professional. They are trained on how to ask questions, what things a person does when they are being dishonest, and how the mind of those planning to abuse someone operates. We dislike any form of stereotyping, but the FBI has profiles of various types of criminals. The school does not violate a person's Fourteenth Amendment rights by keeping a closer eye upon proven or "suspected" hell-raisers.

Every police department in the world has people nearby who operate as informers. Children are always willing to talk to adults, but such a confiding relationship must be nurtured. It takes time to develop a grapevine that works for the good. You can be sure there will always be one that operates in the underworld. Some form of embarrassment may be required with police coming into the building a few times taking someone away in handcuffs. As Machiavelli asserted, a few signal events by the leader early on will eliminate the need for drastic measures later—whether we are talking about school, sports, business, or life. A signal example is just that—a signal! It is accomplished with as big a show as possible when a lesson is being taught. It is why the police don't like it when you pull off the road into a parking lot when you are stopped for speeding. The bigger the display, the less people who will run afoul of the law; they would rather you be as close to the busy road as possible—even blocking traffic and pissing off as many people as possible. Watch *Law and Order* as the detectives go right in to the suspect professor's classroom and start reading him his rights as they cart him off in front of all his students. The bigger the show, the better.

Adults learn quickly from the reactions they observe by their people in leadership positions, as do children. It is why teachers are often passive supervisors of the hallways and cafeteria. When they did turn something into a "federal case," sending numerous people to the office, perhaps it did not always appear to them that the people in the office were taking things as seriously as they were. Eventually, they take the view of the victims: why bother making a fuss? The victimized child also learns quickly to keep his mouth shut or face worse violence. Guidance folks will cringe, but the Bullies must be made to fear something, and the thought of being taken out of the building in handcuffs is an act that will only really need to happen perhaps once or twice. It will have an amazing effect on the "bad guys."

Here's an idea for all of you school principals out there: you that are too chicken to cancel the powder-puff bowl...

Go to the football coach like my old choir teacher did when she needed to have more boys in the choir. After a few football players showed up in the back row singing baritone and bass, boys were knocking down the door to join the choir, and so were the girls. Tell the football coach, and the baseball, basketball, and wrestling coaches, that you would like to see his guys be a mentor to the incoming ninth-grade boys. If they have any problems, they can chat with the athlete. No bully will go near the former victims. They will be worried about what might happen to themselves. There's a YouTube video out there as you read this about some high school football players who "adopted" a girl with Down's syndrome because she was being picked on by the other kids. She now eats lunch with the guys, and she refers to them as "my boys." She's on the sideline at all the games. No one bothers her anymore.

Remember the bus ride that included younger and older students? Come up with big brothers and sisters for each of the kindergarten and first graders on the bus. Give out citizenship awards and a lot of recognition to these big brothers and sisters. Pick a few troublemakers to serve as big brothers and sisters. School troublemakers react well to being assigned something positive. Witness the television shows that have convicts training dogs, for example—the result is always a positive one. Watch the problem go away without bringing in expensive programs that always sound good after the fact but are too often based on the false equivalence logic fallacy, where we all are supposed to be nice to one another—a wonderfully altruistic notion, but you won't reach that level of humanity in your lifetime. Do it for window dressing, but bring in some police personnel to speak about being proactive, establishing grapevines of informants, and allowing students to assist in the supervision process by being mentors and big brothers/sisters. You don't want those police? You didn't hesitate to suggest that school people pack heat, remember? Research has shown that when there is a culture of confronting and telling on the bullies, the cowardly bully disappears.

Working together, we can minimize this terrible nightmare of daily abuse for children. It is not so much about money as it is about commitment. Also, the health teacher can make this an important aspect of the curriculum. Let's brainstorm and get everyone involved, including, first, students, then custodians, bus drivers, administrators, teachers, and parents. Sometimes, great ideas can come from unexpected places. Remember the Hummer commercial, when all of these bigger people were sitting around the table trying to come up with a new idea, and the little guy who delivers the office mail says to them, "Why don't you make a small one?" As he leaves the room, the brilliant people around the table stare at the guy, speechless. Enter the H2—a smaller Hummer. Seek input from everyone. You already know that the old folks are going to say that you need to "kick some more butt like in the good old days," but there might be some effective ideas that are also not costly.

Bullying is never going away. The schools must create adult supervisors that are aware of the context in which they work and are proactive with their strategies so that acts of bullying never happen in the first place. More importantly, justice must prevail—both for the victim and for the perpetrator. School district–wide anti-bullying programs, often instituted after the fact, are of high quality and important. But steps taken in advance and an honest appraisal of the zeitgeist in which the children live and learn must be made. As asserted, a school district is being dishonest when it says, "Bullying does not occur here." They are merely protecting the institution, as the Catholic Church and Penn State recently were accused of doing, rather than putting the children's welfare first. Hokie Pride was an embarrassment, given the depth of the tragedy.

We repeat: bullying is never going away. It's happening in your workplace, in the news, and on your street. Schools are a microcosm of the greater community. How much civility do you see these days? Children are fast learners. Let's resolve to teach them something different. All of us can help in this process.

Those of you in the public schools and the media generally frown on any mention of the Bible to express a point, but this one is worth mentioning. It comes from a Bible book you never read, and one your minister and Sunday school teacher never mentioned. The name of the book is hard to pronounce, and the book—Habbakuk—is not very long. Read the first and second chapters.

Like us, Habakkuk is talking to God and asking him if he is really watching all of this terrible behavior on the part of the "bad guys" that is going on in the world. (Unlike the other prophets, Habakkuk is scolding God!) He must not be, reasons Habakuk; otherwise, God would step in and fix this mess that the world finds itself in. It's really rather unique, because in most other books of the Bible, the various prophets are much more respectful of who they are addressing when it comes to God. Habakkuk reasons to God in a somewhat critical and demanding tone.

Since you folks that run the schools are in charge, let's put you in the driver's seat with the ability to change things. Let's put the children in the role of the questioner—Habakkuk. Don't you see what is happening here, adults? When are you going to fix this? When is the victim going to get justice? The "bad guys" are laughing at your stupid rules and the guidance counselor's "magic circles." If it's not going away, you must not really be paying attention, God, but simply going through the motions with supervisors who want order, but not necessarily justice.

Happily for Habakkuk, God gives him a satisfactory answer, beginning by telling him that he can "write this down"—it's a guarantee that it will be dealt with—and since God never has shown that he can lie, Habakuk and all of us have faith that real justice is coming, in the spiritual sense. Can you folks running the schools really make that guarantee? More decontextualized supervision and bigger football coaches yelling louder in the hallways and guidance counselors who make everyone sit down and talk things out are not fixing the problem.

....

Incentive Pay???

I put three question marks there for a reason, because as it relates to bullying in the schools, it becomes an amazingly good idea; but under the present zeitgeist, it's a terrible idea, and I will try to explain to you, closet Tea Party folks out there—likely to no avail. The math teacher and the reading teacher can show progress—or the lack of same—each year by way of the legendary multiple choice test. However, I'm sure even the most miserly of you folks out there would agree that *all* teachers in a school should have a shot at earning this extra compensation.

Well, work with me. Let's at least pretend you do. Tell me how the art teacher, the music teacher, and the physical education teacher will demonstrate progress. Here's how the art teacher will be having kids memorize inane facts about artists and art museums instead of doing artistic things and expressing one's creativity and inner thought through his art. Is that what you want your kids to be doing in art, because for that trt teacher to get extra compensation, she has to show progress in something that can be easily quantified? If it's not going to be that way—in other words, if the art teacher's ability to receive incentive pay will be tied to some form of subjective judgment, then the math teacher will want to be judged in the same qualitative way as the art teacher for the whole process to work.

Imagine your child taking the art exam…23. Vincent Van Gogh cut off his ear in (a) 1742, (b) 1875, (c) 1903, (d) none of these.

Art, when reduced to a quantifiable, *Who Wants to Be a Millionaire*–type multiple choice test will cease to be art, as we all take another giant step toward collective cretinism. Of course, the only kids allowed to actually "do" art will be the wealthy kids whose parents have the money to send them to a private academy where they don't even have to take all these stupid standardized tests that keep the testing industry rich.

Same with music class folks…41. Which of these composers was deaf? (a) Mozart, (b) Debussy, (c) Beethoven, (d) Paul Mc Cartney…

Say good-bye to music, folks. No more improvisational playing of tambourines and woodblocks and triangles by your first grader because the person left to teach "music" will be giving spelling tests and true-false quizzes.

Physical dducation? Forget about fitness; we have to review for the test…Circle whether each is true or false…5. There is 90 feet between the bases in softball.

By now, if we were in court, the other side would stipulate and ask that learned counsel not produce any further examples, lest he insult our intelligence.

Okay, hopefully, the point was made. *But*, let's suppose the incentive pay was tied to the eradication of bullying in our school…or perhaps, reducing the total incidents of bullying this year by 25%. This would be a goal that would be easy for all of us to share in. The result would be a safer, friendlier school, and one that is more scholarly—more conducive to learning, if you will. Sound crazy? How many schools in the entire world—all of which have bullying whether they admit it or not—have ever thought of ending bullying for good in the school with a plan like this? Do you think we would all have a shared interest in improving the workplace and making people more focused on learning and respectful of one another?

Those pesky test scores might see a bump of some kind in an incentive program tied to the eradication of bullying. Certainly, the supervision skills of seemingly intelligent but decontextualized professionals would improve dramatically. Peer pressure would make sure that everyone is out in the hall between classes, carefully watching things. How about including some money for the students who give information that leads to the "arrest and conviction" of the usual perpetrators?

We mention the work of Stan Davis, who seems to understand the principal idea of this book when he wrote this: "School staff need to believe that it is their job to forge genuine relationships with students. They can set a goal that each student should have a positive relationship—and we would add trusting relationship so that the child will tell the adult anything—with at least two staff members."

"In that way," posits Davis, "the staff members model the behavior that everyone here is important and students get a clear message." He further believes that when staff members have to discipline students for acts of aggression, the consequences they employ will work better because they have a meaningful staff-student relationship with some students. This is what *supervision in context* is all about. If an adult really knows the kids and has taken the time to forge a genuine trusting relationship, the supervision becomes proactive rather than reactive, and the children, by trusting and confiding in the adults, will make sure that the adults really know what is happening out there. Police establish these kinds of relationships in their community. They can find out things behind the scenes ahead of time that the formal process cannot. The same holds true in the schools. Then supervision will finally be less decontextualized, and bullying may finally begin to disappear.

Let's conclude with a beautiful poem by a student. Can you feel this girl's pain? Do you get the sense that she has tried turning the other cheek, maintaining a straight face, acting in a kindly way toward her enemies, yet it never, ever ends? She is not alone. Maybe we can fix it. Let's try.

Everyday It Happens
Kathleen Kiker
Every time I speak, another person hates me,
Every time they answer, I must forgive again.
Every time I listen, I suppress my angry comments,
Every time I hear them, I brush away the tears.
Everywhere I go, I am a nameless victim,
Everywhere I hide, they find me once again.
Every time they see me, I put a happy face on,
Every time they leave me, the tears roll down my cheeks.
Every night I'm sleeping, I dream of faceless horrors,
Every day I'm living, I wish it were not so.
*From poetry on bullying online...selected from "Writing Circle"

About the Author

Dr. Dan Chandler has been a highly successful educator for forty-six years. He has taught in the elementary grades, the middle school, high school, and he has taught aspiring teachers at the college and graduate levels. Additionally, he was a successful high school and middle school principal for eighteen years in several settings in Pennsylvania. He has also coached a variety of sports at the high school and college levels.

Eschewing the ivory tower, Dan has published numerous pragmatic and easily readable articles for teachers, coaches, administrators, and parents. He has a doctoral degree from Temple University and three master's degrees and is a member of the American College of Forensic Examiners, where he has provided litigation support for plaintiffs in their issues with schools. His approach is improvisational and humanistic, and one that is specifically *heart first*, emphasizing effectiveness over efficiency and the importance of "doing the right thing" as opposed to "doing things right" if the two ideas clash.

In Dr. Chandler's view, standardized tests have one purpose by design—to discourage children and make them lower their aspirations so the country will be able to have a steady stream of workers happy to do the ever-increasing number of menial jobs for low pay and few benefits. The powers that be, in Dan's opinion, want less students aspiring to college rather than more. He urges discernment and contextualized supervision of students as the way to control the bullying in schools, which usually occurs close to the adults, yet goes unseen and seldom makes it possible for the victims to get justice. His daily approach to everything he attempts comes from Paul's words to the Christian congregation in Rome: "Don't be conquered by the evil, but conquer the evil with good" (Rom. 12:21).

We hope you find the information informative and eye-opening as to what the school zeitgeist as regards bullying is really like and some thoughts about how this problem that is not going away can be more effectively managed.